101 DAYS OF ABSOLUTE VICTORY

Powerful Devotions and Declarations
of Faith to Energize Your Life

By
Billy Joe Daugherty

Harrison
Tulsa, OK

09 08 07 06   10 9 8 7 6 5 4 3 2 1

101 Days of Absolute Victory
Powerful Devotions and Declarations of Faith to Energize Your Life
ISBN 13: 978-1-57794-820-9
ISBN 10: 1-57794-820-3
(Previously ISBN 1-56267-540-0)
Copyright © 2006 by Daugherty Ministries, Inc.
7700 S. Lewis Ave.
Tulsa, OK 74136

Published by Harrison House, Inc.
P.O. Box 35035
Tulsa, Oklahoma 74153

Introduction

Victory is God's plan for every person living today. Mankind was created to have dominion on the earth. Through His death on the Cross, Jesus Christ regained the authority that Adam lost in the garden of Eden. Jesus has given you grace and righteousness so you might reign on the earth. You were born again a winner—a triumphant one.

Knowing what Jesus has done for you and in you will change your life. He destroyed the power of the devil. (1 John 3:8.) He disarmed the wicked demon spirits. (Col. 2:15.) His resurrection has made possible a resurrection in you. You have been raised from death to life, from defeat to victory.

Agree with God by saying what His Word says. As you do, you will rise up to live on the level of your confession. You are what God says you are. You can do what He says you can do. God has plans for you that are beyond your wildest dreams. He has planned for you to live in victory!

Billy Joe Daugherty

— 1 —

Stronger Each Day

How blessed is the man whose strength is in You,
In whose heart are the highways to Zion!
They go from strength to strength,
Every one of them appears before God in Zion.

PSALM 84:5,7 NASB

God says you are blessed because your strength is in Him. *"The Lord is the strength of my life..."* (Ps. 27:1). God's own power dwells in you. You have His ability, His force, His might, and His energy. All of God's strength is yours.

You are daily increasing in strength. Every moment you are getting stronger and are going from one degree of strength to another. God's Word is what builds you up and gives you strength.

God has not given you a defeated attitude, one that cowers in fear, but rather He has given you a "spirit of power." (2 Tim. 1:7.)

When you made Jesus the Lord of your life, you exchanged your weakness for His strength. As a result, you are now strong in the Lord and in the power of His might. (Eph. 6:10.)

You have been strengthened with might by God's Spirit in your inner man. (Eph. 3:16.) Resurrection power is flowing through you by the Holy Spirit.

You have an anointing from God that breaks every yoke of bondage. (Isa. 10:27.)

You never have to be afraid again because you know who you are. You know who Jesus is and what He has done for you. The Word makes all the difference.

You have realized that meekness is not weakness, but rather a total dependence on Jesus. He is strong. The government is upon His shoulder. (Isa. 9:6.)

DECLARATION OF FAITH

I am strong in the Lord and in the power of His might.
Every day I live, God's strength is increasing in me.
The Spirit of God rests upon me in the fullness
of His power. Weakness is a thing of the past.

— 2 —

Victory Through Our
Lord Jesus Christ

But thanks be to God, who gives us the victory
through our Lord Jesus Christ.

1 CORINTHIANS 15:57

Instill this mighty truth into your heart, soul, and body: *You have victory through Jesus Christ!* Yes, victory has been given to you. That means you have total and complete victory in every area of your life and over *all* the power of the adversary.

You have absolute victory in Jesus Christ. Victory is a gift you receive in Him the moment you accept Jesus as your Lord and Savior. Think it, dream it, talk it, and you will live it.

The Word of God is filled with promises guaranteeing God's help and provision for you. As you continually fill your mind with these blessings, you will rise up and walk in the realm of victory. Victory is already yours; you don't have to *try* and get it. You already have it! The knowledge of the truth sets you free from the limitations of your old life. You are liberated to walk in the light of the new creation.

Your victory is not dependent upon educational degrees, Sunday school certificates, or perfect attendance at worship services. Victory is yours because of what Jesus has done. The work of redemption was completed through His suffering, His death, and His resurrection. "The work" is finished. The thing for you to do is believe it. Just consider that it is done.

Continual confession of what you have in Christ builds a fortress in your mind. It establishes a pattern of response to situations and circumstances. God performs His Word (Jer. 1:12), so speak the Word and watch Him perform it in your life.

DECLARATION OF FAITH

I have victory through Christ. Everything I do is successful through Jesus. God gives me victory everywhere I go. I cannot lose for I have victory through my Lord Jesus Christ.

— 3 —

Wanting Nothing

*My brethren, count it all joy when you
fall into various trials, Knowing that the testing of your
faith produces patience. But let patience have its perfect
work, that you may be perfect and complete, lacking
nothing.*

JAMES 1:2-4

You can rejoice in the midst of temptations! The reason you can rejoice is because God gives you the ability and power to overcome every temptation you face. He will never abandon you during a period of trial and testing.

The grace of God is sufficient to enable you to meet every obstacle victoriously. Let joy be your source of strength. (Neh. 8:10.) It is a very high form of faith. Joy releases the power of God to work in your behalf.

God tells you to rejoice in the very face of tests, trials, and temptations. By doing so, you are releasing your faith,

5

and the power of God goes forth to overcome any barrier. Your rejoicing is *in God*, not in the test, trial, or temptation.

The reason many have not taken advantage of these verses is because they has been misunderstood. People could not reconcile rejoicing over tests, trials, and temptations. If someone continually gives thanks *for* temptations, they actually open the door for more tests and trials to come.

Learn to thank God *in* the situation for His grace that causes you to overcome and not *for* the situation. Praise God for what He has done for you instead of glorifying the devil for his attacks. There is a line between the two attitudes that is of the utmost importance.

As you rejoice in God's help to overcome the temptation, you will be standing on the Word in faith. This is called patience or steadfastness. As you are patient and consistent, God promises you will be perfect and entire, wanting nothing. (James 1:4.)

DECLARATION OF FAITH

I am patient. I rejoice in all situations, for I know
that God perfects me and supplies everything I need.
I lack no good thing. God is Lord over every
trial and temptation that tries to come my way,
and He causes me to triumph in every situation.

— 4 —

Abundant Life

*"The thief does not come except to steal, and to kill,
and to destroy. I have come that
they may have life, and that they may
have it more abundantly."*

Abundant life is God's phrase for the "good life." *Abundant* means "excess, more than enough, bounteous, rich, profuse, extravagant, fully enough, and lavish." This is the type of life God has planned for every believer and that includes *you*. He wants your life to be blessed—abundant, prosperous, and successful.

The devil is the thief, the killer, and the destroyer. God is the blesser, the giver, and the abundant one. Don't get God and the devil mixed up. They are totally different with opposite motives concerning your welfare. God is for you. The devil is against you. However, since God is for you, the devil can't stand against you.

Jesus came into the world so we would experience the life of God, which is abundant, full, and ample. He came to the earth to *give* life to you, not to *take* it from you.

Jesus died on the Cross and was resurrected from the dead so you could live an abundant life. You receive resurrection, or abundant life, when you become born again.

You were not reborn to barely get along. Your heavenly Father does not take pleasure in seeing His children living in poverty. Realize this: God wants you to enjoy His riches in glory right now. He loves you and does not plan for your failure. Instead, He plans for you to succeed. He plans for you to experience eternal, abundant life *now!* And this life is always more than enough!

DECLARATION OF FAITH

I live abundantly in Christ Jesus. He is my Shepherd, and I do not want. No good thing is withheld from me. God has blessed me with every spiritual blessing in the heavenly places in Christ Jesus.

— 5 —

Redeemed

Christ has redeemed us from the curse of the law,
having become a curse for us....
that the blessing of Abraham might come upon
the Gentiles in Christ Jesus, that we might
receive the promise of the Spirit through faith....
And if you are Christ's, then you are Abraham's
seed, and heirs according to the promise.

GALATIANS 3:13,14,29

As a born-again believer, you are stamped with the mark of the blessing because you are Abraham's seed. The anointing of God is upon you, and He favors you!

With favor comes insight, wisdom, revelation, and ideas. Joseph received supernatural revelation on how to manage and oversee the storage of grain. That was a major engineering feat. In the same way, the blessing of God will enable you to receive insight for whatever area of life in which you are involved.

Years ago, when Sharon and I first started out in ministry, there was a young man in our hometown who decided to open a men's clothing store. There already were two or three men's stores that seemed to have a corner on the market. Even though this young man didn't know how to match his own socks, his dream came from God.

In a matter of a few years, his store became the number one men's clothing store in all of Southwest Arkansas. How did he gain an edge over the other stores? He loved on every person who came into his store, he talked with them, and he ministered to them. He prayed in the Holy Spirit continually, and he was diligent. When he went to market, he made his selections while praying in the Holy Spirit.

What God did for this young man, He will do for you as you seek Him and realize that in Christ, you are Abraham's seed and an heir to all the promises of God.

DECLARATION OF FAITH

I have been redeemed from the curse of the law.
I am stamped with the anointing and favor
of the Lord. Everything I put my hand to prospers because I
am of the seed of Abraham.

— 6 —

World Overcomer

For whatever is born of God overcomes the world. And
this is the victory that has overcome the world—our
faith.
Who is he who overcomes the world,
but he who believes that Jesus is the Son of God?

1 JOHN 5:4,5

Most people have associated overcoming with achievement, assuming that they gradually grow into the position of being overcomers. Notice the verse again. Who does it say is an overcomer? *"...He who believes that Jesus is the Son of God."* This means every Christian. From the very moment you are born again, you are an overcomer!

You are a child of God and have been born into the family of overcomers. Every born-again child of God is an overcomer. You are no exception. You are as much of an overcomer as any other believer.

11

It is up to you to simply accept your God-appointed position. Agree with God, and never again confess that you are a failure or a loser. You are a born overcomer. You are, by your new nature, an overcomer. See victory in every area of your life.

Jesus is the true overcomer, and He now lives in you. Your faith in His life in you is your victory. Believe and confess that Jesus lives His life in you and you live your life in Him.

Faith is the victory. Acceptance and recognition of Jesus and His finished work always produce confidence. You can boldly say that you overcome temptations and all forms of evil.

Stand on the rights and privileges you have in Christ. Never forget that God dwells on the inside of you. Acknowledge and accept what He says about you.

DECLARATION OF FAITH

I am a world overcomer! I overcome the lust of the flesh, the lust of the eyes, and the pride of life. Jesus lives in me. Since He is an overcomer, I am an overcomer. What Jesus achieved on the Cross was done so I could live victoriously. My faith in His resurrection is the victory that overcomes the world.

— 7 —

Fellowship With the Father and Son

That which we have seen and heard we declare to you,
that you also may have fellowship with us;
and truly our fellowship is with the Father and
with His Son Jesus Christ.

1 JOHN 1:3

One of the greatest privileges of being saved is fellowship with the Creator of the universe and His Son, the Lord Jesus Christ. There is no greater joy than being in the presence of the Father and Son.

You are only able to fellowship with the Father because of Jesus' suffering for your sins. He was the sacrifice for the sins of mankind. (1 John. 2:2.) There is no sin that the blood of Jesus does not cover.

Strong faith is a product of close fellowship with the Father. Revelation knowledge flows out of intimate communion. As you come to know Him more personally, you will come to better know your victory in Him.

Walking in victory is not achieved simply by following a formula. It is a result of walking in fellowship with your Father and Jesus.

I encourage you to seek after Him. Many people miss it by seeking after success. They don't realize that if you seek after the things of God, you will experience blessings and prosperity. *"But seek first the kingdom of God and His righteousness, and all these things shall be added to you"* (Matt. 6:33).

The Father desires that we fellowship with Him. You do this by reading and meditating on the Word of God and through prayer, which is simply talking to God and listening to what He says back to you. Because of Jesus, we boldly go before the throne of God to fellowship with our Father. (Heb. 4:16.)

DECLARATION OF FAITH

My fellowship is with the Father and His Son, Jesus Christ. Through the blood of Jesus I boldly go to the throne of God to fellowship with Him and seek His face. My fellowship with my heavenly Father is intimate and unbroken.

— 8 —

The Process of
Discipleship

*...He who has begun a good work in you will
complete it until the day of Jesus Christ.*

PHILIPPIANS 1:6

U ntil the day that Jesus returns, He is working in
you and me. Discipleship is a process that we all
go through as we grow in the Lord.

In the Old Testament, Naaman did not want to go
through the process to receive his healing. Second Kings
5:1 says, *"Now Naaman, commander of the army of the
king of Syria, was a great and honorable man in the eye of
his master, because by him the Lord had given victory to
Syria. He was a mighty man of valor, but a leper."*

Naaman went to the prophet Elisha to receive his
healing. Elisha sent his messenger to Naaman with the
message, *"...Go and wash in the Jordan seven times, and
your flesh shall be restored to you, and you shall be clean"*
(2 Kings 5:10). Scripture says Naaman was furious, and he

went away in a rage. After his servants calmed him down, Naaman followed the prophet's instructions and *"...went down and dipped seven times in the Jordan, according to the saying of the man of God; and his flesh was restored like the flesh of a little child, and he was clean"* (2 Kings 5:14).

While some things happen instantaneously, other things have to go through a process before they change. Unfortunately, we live in an age where people think microwave, jiffy, and instant, and they want growth to happen immediately.

In the same way that a child cannot bypass his or her teen years to reach adulthood, you cannot bypass the progression to spiritual maturity that God wants to take you through.

God's goal for your life is that you would grow up to be like Jesus. You can, by choice, commit to the process of being a daily disciple of Jesus Christ. Then, as the whole body of Christ fits together, we will reflect Jesus to the world.

DECLARATION OF FAITH

I commit to a daily time in the Word and in prayer, to godly relationships, and to being a witness of Jesus' love and forgiveness. He who began a good work in me is bringing it to completion. I am becoming like Jesus.

— 9 —

No Condemnation

There is therefore now no condemnation to those who are in Christ Jesus, who do not walk according to the flesh, but according to the Spirit.

ROMANS 8:1

There is glorious liberty in the family of God. Our Father does not condemn us for any past sin. All judgment for sin was placed upon Jesus. As you put your faith in the blood of Jesus, you are cleansed from all sin.

The Spirit of God will convict men and point them to Jesus. The conviction of the Holy Spirit will lead men and women into faith and freedom. The opposite is true of condemnation. It causes people to focus on their sin and away from the forgiveness found in Calvary. Condemnation only leads to fear and bondage. Conviction leads to repentance and life and peace. The difference is profound. One leads to life; the other leads to death.

In your acceptance of Jesus Christ, you have received God's grace and mercy. You are now *in Christ* by virtue of the new birth. There is absolutely no condemnation in Jesus at all. For a brief moment in history, Jesus accepted the sin of the world along with its punishment. Judgment was passed. God is no longer holding the sins of the world against mankind. He is offering reconciliation (forgiveness and pardon) to all who accept His Son.

You are now *in Christ* and can be free from fear and condemnation. You are liberated from guilt—no matter what you have done or where you have been. Since you made Jesus Christ the Lord of your life, there is *no condemnation*.

The truth of Romans 8:1 will keep you singing the rest of your life. Think on it. Talk about it. Most of all, act on it. Since you are not condemned, you have no need to condemn others. What a freedom to see others reconciled to God and to tell them the Good News!

DECLARATION OF FAITH

*There is no condemnation in me. I refuse all guilt
and shame over past sins and failures.
I am free in Jesus for I have received God's grace.*

— 10 —

Anointed for Service

Jesus said to them again, "...As the Father
has sent Me, I also send you."
And when He had said this, He breathed on them, and
said to them, "Receive the Holy Spirit."

You are empowered with the Holy Spirit to be a witness to share the saving, healing, and delivering power of Jesus Christ to those in your realm of influence.

I have a friend who is a very successful businessman. He moves in an echelon of leadership where very few people move. He continually gets other executives and business people together in his office and talks to them about God and His ability to transform their lives. He prays with them to receive Jesus Christ as Savior and to be filled with the Holy Spirit with the evidence of speaking in other tongues. He can relate to them because they are in the same business arena.

It's the same way with plumbers, medical profession-
als, construction workers, etc. Since these men and women
are in the same circles, they can easily communicate with
each other because they are on common ground.

The glory of God is going to come in the earth.
However, God needs a vessel to flow through. He wants to
use you right where you are. There are many people who
work with you that are lost and in need of Jesus. The good
news is that God has called you to be an evangelist, pastor,
and apostle in that area.

Victory in life includes allowing God to use you to
reach entire offices, communities, cities, and nations for
His kingdom. If you will sanctify yourself, as Joshua 3:5
says, you will reach entire people groups. *"...Sanctify yourselves, for tomorrow the Lord will do wonders among you."*
Sanctify means "to set aside for holy purposes." God is
going to pour living water through you to others who
desperately need it!

DECLARATION OF FAITH

I am a vessel, sanctified, and empowered through whom God's
living water can be poured out to others. I will share my faith
on the job, in the neighborhood, where I shop, and any place
God directs. I have been saved for God's purposes and plans.

— 11 —

Always Triumphant

*Now thanks be to God who always leads us in triumph
in Christ, and through us diffuses the fragrance of His
knowledge in every place.*

2 CORINTHIANS 2:14

According to this scripture, you *always* triumph in Jesus Christ. Settle this fact in your mind. Begin to confess daily: *I always triumph in Jesus Christ.*

This is the winning attitude to have. It is true positive thinking. If you always triumph, that means you never fail. You never accept defeat as a final verdict. No matter what it looks like or how you feel, when you hold fast to the profession of your faith, God will bring you out on top.

Notice, it is God who causes us to triumph. God will personally accept responsibility for your victory. Stand on the Word, and the Word will put you over. *Any* situation can be changed by the Word of God. David refused to admit defeat in the face of Goliath. God only needed a young lad, a sling, and a stone to miraculously defeat the enemy.

21

A wonderful added blessing to continual triumph is the privilege of manifesting the beautiful fragrance of God's knowledge everywhere you go. God is using you to perfume the earth with His knowledge. You might call it "The Taste of Victory" or "The Essence of Triumph."

The world is in desperate need of knowledge to cope with its current problems. Your constant triumph produces a fragrance that is attractive to people in need. Get ready for opportunities to share your success stories. Tell them it is just part of being *in Christ*.

DECLARATION OF FAITH

I always triumph in Jesus Christ.
I thank God for constant victory.
Every situation I face is an opportunity to manifest the
knowledge of God. I am strong and of a good courage
for I know I always triumph in Jesus Christ.

— 12 —

You Are God's Dream

*But you are a chosen generation, a royal priesthood, a
holy nation, His own special people, that you may
proclaim the praises of Him who called you out of
darkness into His marvelous light.*

1 PETER 2:9

God has great plans for you, and He wants to put
you on display. The reason for this is so that when
people look at you, they will want to serve the
God you serve.

Many people don't know how God feels about them.
They are filled with a sense of worthlessness, aimlessness,
guilt, and condemnation. Their lives are filled with ritual
and routine. They are just making a living and going
through life. They have no sense of where they came from,
why they are here, or where they are headed. They are
living empty, fruitless lives. Many are enslaved to habits
and compulsive thoughts and desires.

There was a young man who grew up in a home where his mother, a very domineering woman, belittled him and his father. He was rejected, alienated, and ostracized at school because he did not fit in with the others. Finally, to get away from home and school, he joined the military where he faced the same problems of rejection and isolation. The only thing he could do was shoot a rifle. He trained well, but eventually was dishonorably discharged.

On November 22, 1963, this young man climbed into the Texas School Book Depository and shot the 35th President of the United States, John F. Kennedy.

It appears that no one ever told Lee Harvey Oswald that he was special or chosen by God. He never learned of the great plans God had for him.

This is the hour for you to know that you are a chosen generation and a royal priesthood so you can help other people know who they are in Christ.

DECLARATION OF FAITH

*Today, I will tell someone they are special because
now I know I am special to God and am chosen
of Him to proclaim His praises.*

— 13 —

You Are Valuable

*For we are His workmanship, created in Christ
Jesus for good works, which God prepared
beforehand that we should walk in them.*

EPHESIANS 2:10

You are God's craftsmanship, His special work.
During creation, God said of everything He
created, "It is good." But when He created man,
male and female, He said of everything He had made, "It is
very good."

Having a revelation of your worth in God will transform your life. Many people lack a sense of worth or value
in their lives. Our society has so focused on the outward
traits of an individual that many people's view of their
value has been distorted. Our culture says people are highly
esteemed if they are beautiful outwardly, if they are intelli-
gent, or if they are talented in music, athletics, or acting.

Some people's potential has been locked up because
they don't value themselves properly. God's view of us is

not based on external traits or abilities. He simply values everybody as special.

When I was in the sixth grade, my feet grew faster than the rest of my body. Mom bought me a pair of Hush Puppy shoes that would fit me for a couple of years. They were two inches longer at the toes and my feet stopped growing, so my shoes looked like an alligator, long with a dip at the end of them! The ridicule and laughs of other students were painful.

When I was singing in the church choir, the other men would always say, "You sit by him today." A warm feeling would go through me! It was obvious that I didn't have the best voice for singing in the choir.

Many people have had to deal with feelings of inferiority because of the putdowns they've received from others. When you understand your value in God, then you will value other people. To walk in victory, you must meditate on what God says about you in His Word. You are a champion. You are God's workmanship. You have been prepared for such a time as this.

DECLARATION OF FAITH

*I am royalty! I am valuable! I am worth the blood
that Jesus Christ shed for me at Calvary!
My value is based on God's view of me.
He believes I am special, and I am.
I see as God sees, and I value others
with the same value.*

— 14 —

Power-filled Witnesses

*"But you shall receive power when the Holy Spirit
has come upon you; and you shall be witnesses
to Me in Jerusalem, and in all Judea and
Samaria, and to the end of the earth."*

ACTS 1:8

The power of God is in you, and nothing can stand against the Spirit of the Lord that resides in you. The power that created the universe is infused in your being. You need not be afraid of anything, or of any man or beast.

The Word of God says the power of the Holy Spirit makes you a witness wherever you go. There is no obstacle too big for the Spirit of God to handle. His wisdom is yours to answer any critic and antagonist. Your lips are fitted with the message of the kingdom of God.

Never be intimidated by any situation. Everyone needs to hear about Jesus, and you have been equipped with the power of God to witness to anyone. When you speak, your words will come forth with power and authority.

See yourself as a mighty soul winner. Make it your lifestyle to preach Jesus and set the captives free. There is no need to apologize or shuffle your feet. You have answered the call by saying, "Here am I, Lord; send me." And He has sent you into the entire world. You can and will do the job.

God has given you all of the equipment you need to go into the harvest fields. Now go in faith.

DECLARATION OF FAITH

The power of the Holy Spirit is upon me to be a witness of Jesus. I am anointed by God to do His work. The Spirit leads and guides me to people who need the Gospel, and He fills my mouth with the words they need to hear.

— 15 —

Rivers of Living Water

Jesus said, "If anyone thirsts,
let him come to Me and drink.
"He who believes in Me, as the Scripture has said,
out of his heart will flow rivers of living water."

On the day of Pentecost, fifty days after Passover, Jesus poured out His Spirit on believers in the upper room, and they began to speak in a new language. Rivers of living water flowed up out of them and they prophesied. This experience—the baptism of the Holy Spirit—is available to every born-again believer.

The origin of the rivers written about in John 7:38 is *the* river that flows from the throne of God. It is the life of God Himself. As we worship God, that river flows. As we speak in other tongues, that river flows. As we prophesy, that river flows. As we speak the Word, that river flows up out of us.

Many people have never experienced the baptism of the Holy Spirit. They have never let the rivers flow out of them. This experience was foreign to me as I was growing up. Later, when I was in college, I realized it was true. It is for today, and it is for all believers.

As a young boy, I swam in the cold waters in Albert Pike at a state park in Arkansas. It didn't matter how hot it was, the temperature of the water always seemed about 38 degrees. When you jumped in, you suddenly came alive. Every fiber of your body was jolted by the coldness of the water.

It's the same way with the baptism of the Holy Spirit. When you receive it, you are filled with a power that affects your entire being. To walk in victory, you must release the refreshing rivers of the life of God that have been deposited inside of you.

DECLARATION OF FAITH

Out of the rivers of God's life in my heart,
my mouth speaks and dominion and authority are released
over sin, sickness and disease, poverty and lack,
and spiritual death.

— 16 —

A Branch of the Vine

"I am the vine, you are the branches.
He who abides in Me, and I in him, bears much fruit;
for without Me you can do nothing."

JOHN 15:5

As a born-again child of God, you are part of Jesus. There is no separation between the branch and the Vine. They grow together and are viewed as one. The branch draws its life from the Vine. You are living in union with Almighty God, and His life is flowing through you *now!*

God's strength has become your strength, and you never need to confess weakness again. To say, "I have no strength" is to deny your relationship with Jesus. All that He is has become yours. Your life is now in Him.

See yourself totally in Jesus. The branch doesn't look to itself for life. It is entirely dependent upon the Vine. It could not exist without the Vine. You can't either. Your confession should always be of what He is in you. Your confession should never be about what you were before you became a part of the Vine.

Feelings have no bearing on the authority of the Word. God's Word is true regardless of how you feel. You may not *feel* as though you are connected to the Vine, but you are. Nothing can separate you from the love of God. (Rom. 8:39.) Be confident about the Word and who it says you are and what you have in Christ.

You have love, joy, and peace. You are more than a conqueror in Christ. (Rom. 8:37.) Abide in Jesus. Confess the Word. Think about who you are Him, and you will bear much fruit.

DECLARATION OF FAITH

Jesus, You are the Vine, and I am the branch.
I am divinely joined to You.
Your life is flowing through me. Everything You are, I am.
Your strength, power, love, joy, and
peace are mine. As a result, I bear much fruit.

— 17 —

God Is Not Mad at You!

God demonstrates His own love toward us, in that
while we were still sinners, Christ died for us.

ROMANS 5:8

God sent His Son to die for mankind when the world was in a sinful state. It's unheard of for a parent to allow his child to die for another individual. Yet, that's exactly what God did for you and me. He did this because of His strong love for us.

You must be important for God to have allowed His only Son to die for you. He saw your potential. He saw what you could be in Christ. Never forget how special you are to Him.

As a result of Jesus' death on the Cross, every day we are being saved from the effects of sin, which include disaster, calamity, tragedy, darkness, and oppression.

The key to receiving the revelation of God's love for us is to *believe*. John 3:16-17 says, *"For God so loved the*

*world that He gave His only begotten Son, that whoever
believes in Him should not perish but have everlasting life.
For God did not send His Son into the world to condemn
the world, but that the world through Him might be
saved."*

When God looks at you, He doesn't see a condemned
sinner; He sees a righteous son or daughter. He sees you—
not through the fallen nature of Adam—but through the
blood of His Son Jesus.

The Bible is filled with promises of what you can be
in Christ. As you will believe, receive, and act on them,
you will walk in the reality of who you are in Christ. God
loves you!

DECLARATION OF FAITH

*My thoughts, words, and actions are lining up with
the beautiful promises of God's Word. God gave
His Son for me that I could become a child of God.
I receive the love of God overflowing in my life.*

— 18 —

Offering Your Body as a Living Sacrifice

I beseech you therefore, brethren, by the mercies of
God, that you present your bodies a living sacrifice, holy,
acceptable to God, which is your reasonable service.

ROMANS 12:1

You can experience a turnaround in your life if you will allow your thinking to be transformed by the daily input of God's Word.

Paul admonished believers in the above scripture. In light of all that God has done for us, we are to give our bodies in service to God as living sacrifices.

In the Old Testament, once a year a sacrifice was offered to God by the high priest. A lamb was killed and laid upon the altar. Its blood covered, or atoned, the sins of the people. In the New Testament, this yearly sacrifice was abolished because of the shed blood of Jesus Christ. His sacrifice paid the price for the sin of mankind once and for all.

Now it's up to us to offer our bodies to God as living sacrifices. No one else can present your body to God but you. Paul said, *"Do not be conformed to this world..."* (Rom. 12:2). *The J. B. Phillips Translation* of this verse says, "Don't let the world around you squeeze you into its own mold, but let God re-mold your minds from within...."

The "world" has lifestyles, mannerisms, and morals that are distinctly different from born-again believers. Unlike the world, a believer's lifestyle, morals, mannerisms, thoughts, words, and actions are to be patterned after Jesus Christ. It is an admonishment from on High that we not be "squeezed" into the world's mold.

Paul said, *"Be transformed...."* This transformation takes place by renewing our minds with God's Word. What God says is what we are to say. We can get our heads "straight" by filling them with God's Word.

DECLARATION OF FAITH

I give my body to serve God and offer it to Him
as a living sacrifice. My mind is being renewed by
the Word of God. My thinking is being rearranged
by the daily input of God's Word.

— 19 —

Daily Surrender

"...O My Father, if it is possible, let this cup pass from
Me; nevertheless, not as I will, but as You will."

MATTHEW 26:39

J esus prayed this prayer of total submission to the
Father in the garden of Gethsemane before His arrest
and crucifixion. He did not want to drink from the cup
that was placed before Him. He prayed that the crucifixion
(the Cross) would pass from Him. He did not want to experience the suffering, humiliation, the nails, the crown of
thorns, and the rejection. However, Jesus ended His prayer
with, *"...Not as I will, but as You will."*

You can follow along a path with the right intent in
your heart, but it is important that you surrender your will
to God every day, for your path may lead you to a place that
you don't want to go. However, you must make a decision
to do whatever God tells you to do.

On January 8, 1981, I was praying about where our
church could meet when it suddenly became crystal clear:

"Tink Wilkerson's Auto Mart." That was 10:30 at night, it was 32 degrees outside, and I had my pajamas on. I immediately put on a coat and drove to 4400 South Sheridan in Tulsa. I stepped out of my car, pointed to the building, and called it into the ministry.

Over the next few days, as I shared my vision, I received mixed responses. Many people could not comprehend worshiping God in a car dealership with the lifts, grease pits, and showroom windows!

Eventually, I was interviewed by a reporter from a local newspaper who wrote a story about the car dealership. The young lady wrote, "Come to Victory if you need a lift!" Thousands of people came. God made a way for us. It was a great beginning.

You may be in a situation where you know what to do in your heart, but your mind is fighting you. Surrender to God and do whatever He says. Not only will you be blessed, but others will also be blessed because of your submission and obedience to God.

DECLARATION OF FAITH

I choose to do the Lord's will every day. I hear God's voice through His Spirit and His Word, and I obey Him. God's blessings overtake me as I do the will of God.

— 20 —

Treasure In...
Treasure Out!

Do not be conformed to this world, but be transformed
by the renewing of your mind, that you may prove what
is that good and acceptable and perfect will of God.

ROMANS 12:2

When you accept Jesus Christ as your Lord and Savior, the life of God comes into your heart, or spirit being, and you become a new creature in Christ. (2 Cor. 5:17.) Your head, however, is still full of the same old thoughts you had before giving your life to Christ.

When you think the wrong, or sinful, thoughts, your body will follow in that direction. To continue living in sin when your heart is filled with the life of God only brings guilt, condemnation, and frustration.

Unfortunately, this is where many Christians are today. They know what is right, but their unrenewed thinking leads them in a wrong direction.

The mind is a battlefield for many. Whatever you think about constantly will eventually be acted out in your life. You cannot put garbage in your mind and expect something good to come out. If you want a different output, then you have to change the input.

If the life you are experiencing is not what you want, then you must increase the amount of time you spend reading, hearing, studying, and meditating on God's Word. The light of God's Word will drive darkness out of your life.

Some people try to quit sinning—lying, stealing, lusting, and getting angry, to name a few areas of challenge of the old nature. Sometimes they ask their pastor to pray their old sinful nature out of them, but no amount of praying will work. If their minds aren't renewed with God's Word, they'll still think wrong thoughts and act out what they are thinking. It's only by putting so much of the Word inside of you that sin will quit you. This is the only way to overcome your old, sinful nature.

DECLARATION OF FAITH

I am filling myself up with the Word of God so sin will quit me. The light of God's Word is driving all darkness out of me. I put God's Word in my eyes, ears, mind, and heart and speak it from my lips. Anger, fear, loneliness, and all of my old nature are all removed by the power of Jesus inside of me.

— 21 —

Winning the Battle in Your Mind

For though we walk in the flesh,
we do not war according to the flesh.
For the weapons of our warfare are not carnal
but mighty in God for pulling down strongholds,
Casting down arguments and every high thing that exalts
itself against the knowledge of God, bringing every
thought into captivity to the obedience of Christ.

2 CORINTHIANS 10:3-5

Your mind is the arena of your faith fight. Faith grows in your spirit by hearing God's Word. (Rom. 10:17.) The righteous live by faith. They are saved, delivered, and healed by faith. The faith fight takes place between your two ears!

Fill your thought life with the Word of God. This is called "renewing your mind." (Rom. 12:2.) Isaiah 26:3 says, *"You will keep him in perfect peace, whose mind is stayed on You, because he trusts in You."*

In Philippians 4:8 AMP, Paul tells us exactly what we are to think on to be free from worry and anxiety:

> ...*whatever is true, whatever is worthy of reverence and is honorable and seemly, whatever is just, whatever is pure, whatever is lovely and lovable, whatever is kind and winsome and gracious, if there is any virtue and excellence, if there is anything worthy of praise, think on and weigh and take account of these things [fix your minds on them].*

Instead of confessing symptoms, a negative medical diagnosis, or the details of a difficult situation, speak the promises of God regarding your situation. Negative thoughts have no choice but to leave your mind.

DECLARATION OF FAITH

I am healthy and whole in my thought life because I take daily doses of God's Word and meditate on His promises. God's Word is true, and it is truth in my life.

— 22 —

Faith Without Works
Is Dead

What does it profit, my brethren, if someone says he has
faith but does not have works? Can faith save him?
If a brother or sister is naked and destitute of daily food,
And one of you says to them, "Depart in peace, be
warmed and filled," but you do not give them the things
which are needed for the body, what does it profit?

JAMES 2:14-16

The spirit of faith involves believing, receiving, and confessing the promises of God. That's one side of the faith coin. The other side is that there must be corresponding actions to what you believe, which involves obedience to what God has told you to do. To tell someone to be warmed and filled and not provide for the individual's practical needs is of no benefit.

This is why we started the Tulsa Dream Center—to put feet to our faith and help the poor in our city in numerous ways: food and clothing distribution; dental, medical, and legal services; educational services; recreational opportunities; and spiritual enrichment opportunities.

James goes on to say, *"...faith by itself, if it does not have works, is dead"* (James 2:17).

Years ago, Sharon and I were youth directors in the church where Kenneth E. Hagin's Campmeetings began. Fred Price was a guest speaker at the church and asked everyone to imagine a starving man who had a plate of well-prepared food in front of him. The man's confession was, "I believe if I eat this food I will not die." There was nothing wrong with his belief system, but there were no corresponding actions to his belief. He never touched the food. On the second and succeeding days, this scene was repeated, and eventually the man died because he never ate any food.

Like that starving man, you can repeatedly say, "I believe," but if there is no follow-through or corresponding actions, you will be defeated.

DECLARATION OF FAITH

I am putting corresponding actions to my faith—
to God's promises that I am believing and speaking.
I choose to be a doer of the Word and not just a hearer.

— 23 —

Greater Works

"Most assuredly, I say to you, he who believes in Me,
the works that I do he will do also; and greater works
than these he will do, because I go to My Father.
"And whatever you ask in My name, that I will do,
that the Father may be glorified in the Son."

JOHN 14:12,13

J esus said that you will not only do what He did, you
will also do greater things. This promise is for all
believers and not just the twelve apostles. Notice that
verse 12 says, *"He who believes...."* That includes any born-
again person who believes God's Word.

Think of all the miracles Jesus performed while He was
on the earth. Now think of those miracles in light of John
14:12. In other words, see yourself doing what Jesus did.

See yourself speaking to the blind man and commanding him to see. See yourself commanding the paralytic to
rise and walk in the name of Jesus. See yourself casting out
devils and praying for withered hands to be restored.

The Scripture says you will do the same works Jesus did. If you were told you would be taking the place of another person in a factory or business operation, you would inquire about that individual's job responsibilities. You would see yourself doing that job. This is exactly what Jesus has called you to do.

You have been called to fulfill the ministry of Jesus on the earth today. Don't despair; Jesus guarantees you His support. You can ask the Father anything in His name, and it will be done for you. (John 16:23.)

Stand in the authority you have in the name of Jesus. Then be bold and imitate Jesus in everything that He did. As you envision yourself ministering as Jesus did, you will.

DECLARATION OF FAITH

I do the same works that Jesus did and greater ones too. Whatever I ask the Father in Jesus' name will be granted so the Father may be glorified.

— 24 —

Divine Protection

He who dwells in the secret place of the Most High
shall abide under the shadow of the Almighty.
I will say of the Lord, "He is my refuge and my fortress;
my God, in Him I will trust.

PSALM 91:1,2

There is a secret place in God that is available to every person, and there is only one way to get there—through faith in the blood of Jesus Christ.

When you accept Jesus Christ as your Lord and Savior, He gives you eternal life. You enter into the family of God. You become an heir of God and a joint heir with Jesus Christ. (Rom. 8:17.) You are no longer an outcast. Regardless of your age, color, nationality, or gender, you have access into the Father's presence through Jesus Christ.

However, to receive Psalm 91 benefits, you must meet Psalm 91 conditions. The conditions are laid out in verses 1 and 2, and the benefits are laid out in the rest of the chapter.

The first condition: You must make the Most High God your dwelling place and abide in Him. When you are dwelling in the secret place of the Most High, you are in vital union with Jesus. You are submitted to His lordship and authority. Your faith has been linked to His light.

The second condition: *"I will say of the Lord, 'He is my refuge and my fortress; my God, in Him I will trust.'"* What you say will put you over or put you under. Your words rule your life because you are either speaking life or death. (Prov. 18:21.)

When the angel Gabriel told Mary, the young virgin, that she would conceive, she made a profound statement. She said, *"...Let it be to me according to your word..."* (Luke 1:38). The miracle of the virgin birth was based on these words.

The same will happen with you. As you agree with the Word of God, you will see it come to pass in your life.

DECLARATION OF FAITH

The Lord is my refuge and my fortress, my God in whom I trust. I dwell in the secret place of the Most High, and I abide under the shadow of the Almighty. He guards, guides, delivers, and directs my life!

— 25 —

You Shall Never Die

Jesus said to her, "I am the resurrection and the life.
He who believes in Me, though he may die, he shall live.
"And whoever lives and believes in Me shall never die...."

JOHN 11:25,26

The moment you received Jesus as your Lord and Savior, your old life passed away and a new life came into existence. In essence, you had a "death" experience. *"For you died, and your life is hidden with Christ in God"* (Col. 3:3).

Ephesians 2:5-6 says that when you became alive in Christ (when you became born again), you were raised up to sit with Christ in heavenly places.

One aspect of your born-again experience is to be delivered from the fear of death because Jesus destroyed *"...him who had the power of death, that is, the devil"* (Heb. 2:14). As a result, you have absolute assurance that when you leave your physical body, you will be with Jesus in heaven.

The Apostle Paul summed up the way Christians should feel about death: *"For to me, to live is Christ, and to die is gain"* (Phil. 1:21). Think about it. Born-again Christians no longer have to fear death. We can live fearlessly. We can live in peace because we know that we are divinely protected from evil; and at the same time, there is no underlying torment about eternal death.

Christians really never die. They simply change clothes. They take off their earth suits and put on their heavenly attire. There doesn't have to be any sorrow, fear, or depression about death, for it is simply crossing over into the glory of heaven.

DECLARATION OF FAITH

*I am crucified with Christ, nevertheless I live,
yet Christ lives in me. I have been raised with Christ
and sit with Him in heavenly places. I am eternally
alive in Jesus. Although my body may be laid to rest
in the grave, my spirit is alive forever in Jesus.*

— 26 —

Freedom From Fear

For [God] made [Jesus] who knew no sin to be sin for us,
that we might become the righteousness of God in Him.

2 CORINTHIANS 5:21

Jesus brought you into right relationship with God. Because of His atoning work on the Cross, you are now accepted into God's family as if you had never sinned. When you know that you are right with God through faith in what Jesus did, then fear and anxiety have no place in your life.

In His death, burial, and resurrection, Jesus took your sin so you could have His righteousness. The moment you believe in Jesus Christ and accept Him as your Savior and Lord, you are made the righteousness of God in Christ. (2 Cor. 5:21.)

Many years ago when we were traveling in ministry, the Lord dealt with me to preach on righteousness every night in a church. You see, when people feel condemned, unworthy, and unrighteous, their faith won't work. They won't receive healing in their marriages, in their bodies, or in their finances. A chief elder of this church sat on the front row during the services. However, he did not agree with the teaching on righteousness. While I was preaching, he would say aloud, "No, no."

Thank God that the entrance of His Word gives light. (Ps. 119:130.) About the fourth night that I was preaching on righteousness, something went off inside of him; and he said out loud, "Praise God. It's by faith!"

You are righteous in Jesus Christ by faith. An understanding of your righteousness in Him will free you of all fear and enable you to boldly go into the throne room of God. (Heb. 4:16.)

DECLARATION OF FAITH

I receive the great exchange of God's gift of righteousness that was provided for me through Jesus Christ. I have been made the righteousness of God in Him. By faith I accept that. Jesus took my sins and gave me His righteousness.

— 27 —

Never Thirsty

"But whoever drinks of the water that I shall give him will never thirst. But the water that I shall give him will become in him a fountain of water springing up into everlasting life."

JOHN 4:14

Paul said in Ephesians 5:26, *"that He might sanctify and cleanse her with the washing of water by the word."* Water also refers to the Holy Spirit. (John 7:37-39.) As you partake of God's Word and the Holy Spirit, you will be satisfied fully.

People without Christ are thirsting and starving for real life. Their spirits are craving for the eternal because their lives are shallow, empty, and fruitless.

You are a light in a dark place. To those around you, you are a river springing forth in the midst of a desert. The eternal life that is in you is a well of water springing up. It bubbles forth in joy, freedom, and victory.

When you have the Spirit of God bubbling up inside of you, you have a positive outlook on life and are constantly filled with good reports. Instead of speaking death, you are constantly speaking life.

Fear has lost its grip over the dreams of your heart. Like a bird set free, you have no limitations to what you can do. There are no more impossibilities, for your faith has laid hold of eternal life. God is in you.

Jesus has brought you into glorious liberty. Although you may have begun in a dry, thirsty land, the living water that springs forth from your inner being has made the desert blossom like a rose.

Life comes out of you to set the captives free. Healing flows to the sick. Love lifts the downcast, and hope fills the despairing. It is all because Jesus is in you.

DECLARATION OF FAITH

I am a light in dark places. I am a well of the water of life.
As others see me, they too will want the light of God;
and they will want to drink of the water
of life made possible through Jesus.

— 28 —

Your Position in Christ

*But this precious treasure—this light and power that now
shine within us—is held in a perishable container, that is,
in our weak bodies. Everyone can see that the glorious
power within must be from God and is not our own.
We are pressed on every side by troubles, but we are not
crushed and broken. We are perplexed because we don't
know why things happen as they do, but we don't give
up and quit. We are hunted down, but God never
abandons us. We get knocked down, but we get up again
and keep going. These bodies of ours are constantly
facing death just as Jesus did; so it is clear to all that it is
only the living Christ within [who keeps us safe].
Yes, we live under constant danger to our lives
because we serve the Lord, but this gives us
constant opportunities to show forth the power
of Jesus Christ within our dying bodies.*

2 CORINTHIANS 4:7-11 TLB

At one time or another, you may have been hit with
such a hard "blow" that you felt as though you
were down for the count. A friendship ended over

an offense; you or a close family member experienced a serious illness; a financial investment turned sour; you unexpectedly lost your job; or you experienced persecution because of your faith in Jesus Christ.

Keep in mind that when you keep your focus on the Lord in the midst of adversity, your situation will look differently. Too many people only focus on the attack of the enemy and think little about God's ability. However, the more you focus on God and His power, the more you will know that *nothing* is too big for Him.

No matter what comes against you, remember Paul's advice drawn from his experiences of being shipwrecked, beaten, and jailed for the preaching of the gospel: *Don't give up and quit! God will never abandon you. Get up and keep going in His power and strength!*

DECLARATION OF FAITH

"...When I fall, I will arise. When I sit in darkness,
the Lord will be a light to me" (Micah 7:8).
The Lord always causes me to triumph regardless
of what comes against me. (2 Cor. 2:14.)
The Lord is the strength of my life and my deliverer.
(Ps. 27:1; Ps. 18:2.)

— 29 —

Power Over the Enemy

*"Behold, I give you the authority to trample on serpents
and scorpions, and over all the power of the enemy,
and nothing shall by any means hurt you."*

LUKE 10:19

Jesus gave all believers power and authority over the
devil and his demons. You should no longer be
concerned with what the devil is *trying* to do on the
earth. Your focus should be on the things that God has
called *you* to do. Because of the power and authority that
has been invested in you by the head of the church, there is
nothing that can stop what God has called you to do.

People are never blessed by hearing what the devil
has done. Faith comes by hearing the Word of God. As you
talk about the Word and the mighty things that God has
done, people will be encouraged and set free.

It is up to you to stomp on serpents and scorpions
(evil spirits and demons). You can walk on them because of
the shed blood of Jesus and the authority you have been

given. As you use that authority, you have God's Word that "*...nothing shall by any means hurt you.*"

Make this your daily confession: *Nothing shall by any means hurt me or my family.* Expect to live free from accidents, robberies, natural disasters, disease, and the assault of evil men. God's Word is your shield of defense. Put your faith in it for *total immunity* from all the works of the devil.

DECLARATION OF FAITH

In Jesus' name, I have power over all the power
of the enemy. Nothing shall by any means
hurt me or my family. I am immune to evil
by the authority of God's Word.
I rejoice that in the victory that I have
because of the blood of Jesus.

— 30 —

The Kingdom Is Within

"The kingdom of God does not come with observation;
"Nor will they say, 'See here!' or 'See there!'
For indeed, the kingdom of God is within you."

LUKE 17:20,21

What a revelation. You don't have to die to get into the kingdom of God. The kingdom of God is already in you! You don't have to wait to experience the joys of the kingdom; they are here and now!

"For the kingdom of God is not eating and drinking, but righteousness and peace and joy in the Holy Spirit" (Rom. 14:17).

You are the righteousness of God in Jesus Christ. (2 Cor. 5:21.) *"...[You] have peace with God through our Lord Jesus Christ"* (Rom. 5:1).

Kingdom living is a part of reigning in life with Christ Jesus. (Rom. 5:17.) You have been made a king and priest unto God through the blood of Christ. (Rev. 1:5,6.)

Since the kingdom of God is on the inside of you, you don't have to be dominated by situations and circumstances. The Counselor (Isa. 9:6) dwells inside of you, so your direction comes from within rather than from the outside.

The ruler of the kingdom of God is Jesus, and you are His personal friend. Everything He has heard the Father speak, He reveals to you. (John 15:15.) You have inside information about the power that is upholding the universe. You might say you have an "inside track."

Although the kingdom of heaven is invisible to the natural eye, it is nonetheless real and powerful. Kingdoms of the world may rise and fall, but the kingdom of God within you is forever.

DECLARATION OF FAITH

The kingdom of God is within me now. I live in accordance with the laws of God, and I am free from the law of sin and death. (Rom. 8:2.) I experience kingdom righteousness, peace, and joy in the Holy Spirit every day.

— 31 —

The Spirit of the Lord Upon You

"The Spirit of the Lord is upon Me, because He has
anointed Me to preach the gospel to the poor; He has
sent Me to heal the brokenhearted, to proclaim liberty
to the captives and recovery of sight to the blind,
to set at liberty those who are oppressed;
"To proclaim the acceptable year of the Lord."

LUKE 4:18,19

J esus spoke these words as the Son of God. He did miracles and set many people free. It was because the Father had anointed Him with the Spirit of God.

You, too, are anointed by the Holy Spirit. *"But you shall receive power when the Holy Spirit has come upon you..."* (Acts 1:8). God's Spirit has come upon you to give you power to live like Jesus.

The Spirit of God is upon you and teaches you all truth. (John 16:13.) *"But you have an anointing from the Holy*

One, and you know all things" (1 John 2:20). The anointing of God's Spirit gives you revelation, wisdom, and knowledge of the things of God.

Jesus was the Son of God, and you are a son of God as well. You both have the same Father and the same heritage, for you are an heir of God. (Rom. 8:17.) This means that you are to do the same things Jesus did. The same Spirit that was upon Jesus is also upon you.

You can follow in Jesus' footsteps because you have His strength and ability. It is not a man's natural ability or talent that gives victory; it's the power of God that resides within you. *"...Not by might nor by power, but by My Spirit, says the Lord of hosts"* (Zech. 4:6).

Jesus said, *"Most assuredly, I say to you, he who believes in Me, the works that I do he will do also; and greater works than these he will do, because I go to My Father"* (John 14:12). Expect to duplicate the works of Jesus, for He lives in you. You are anointed with the Holy Spirit.

DECLARATION OF FAITH

*The Spirit of the Lord is upon me to preach
the gospel, heal the sick, deliver the oppressed,
and free the captives. As a child of God
I am an heir of God and joint-heir with Jesus.*

— 32 —

Humility

Humble yourselves in the sight of the Lord,
and He will lift you up.

JAMES 4:10

God wants to take you into greater spheres of influence. He wants to increase His blessings in your life. He desires to release power in you that is beyond anything you have ever dreamed or imagined. The only way this can happen is if you humble yourself and let the rivers of God's grace flow into your life.

After you make Jesus the Lord of your life, the greatest blockage to the blessings of God is pride, which includes arrogance, smugness, independence of God, and self-sufficiency.

James 4:7 says, *"Therefore submit to God...."* The real evidence of humility is when you have submitted to what God has told you to do. You have yielded your will to His will.

God wants to exalt you, increase you, and heal you. He wants you to experience happiness in your home and family. He wants you to experience joy and freedom. There is only one way to receive these blessings, and that is to humble yourself.

Why is it so important to have a humble heart? Without it, you will be deceived. You will go in the wrong direction and won't even know it. Your pathway will lead you straight for disaster, and you won't have a clue.

I think about a young man I visited on death row in McAlester State Prison in Oklahoma. As a boy, he had ridden a bus to church in Tulsa. I asked him, "What happened?" He said, "I began running with a gang. My mother told me, 'Don't run with those boys.' I just didn't listen to her."

Jesus is our greatest example of humility because He humbled Himself and obeyed His heavenly Father. Humility always results in obedience, and humbling yourself will result in exaltation.

DECLARATION OF FAITH

I choose to humble myself in the sight of the Lord.
All that I am and all that I have are because of Jesus'
death, burial, and resurrection. He is my example.

— 33 —

Nothing Is Impossible With God

"For with God nothing will be impossible."

LUKE 1:37

As you meditate on the Word of God, you are being infused with faith. Your entire life is being transformed by the power of God's Spirit. You have revelation of the *fact* that God is in you now. Settle it in your heart. Since nothing is impossible with God, then nothing is impossible to you because God lives in your heart.

Everything you are called to do is possible. God will never instruct you to do something that is impossible to Him. There isn't anything that is impossible to God.

Moses faced the Red Sea with a hostile Egyptian army closing in behind him. The situation looked *impossible*. There didn't look like there was any way out. But God had given Moses a rod. It represented His power and authority, His Word. When Moses raised the rod, the sea parted. (Ex. 14:21.) What was impossible for ordinary men became possible to a man who knew his God.

God has given you His power and authority—His Word, His name, and His Spirit. No matter what the obstacle, lift up the rod in Jesus' name and watch the mighty Holy Spirit work miracles.

Mankind has dreamed of living in the miraculous where supernatural feats are possible. It's not just a dream; it's reality! It's not for show or entertainment, but as a witness of God's glory for the lives of those around you. You see, compassion is the motivation behind God's intervention into human affairs. It was because of His love that Jesus spoke those precious words to Mary. It's the Father's heart reaching out to you and me to bring us back into the family.

DECLARATION OF FAITH

Nothing is impossible with God, and nothing is impossible to me because God lives big in me. I can do everything God wants me to do. His divine life in me has given me a victorious attitude.

— 34 —

The Power of Your Words

A man's stomach shall be satisfied from the fruit of his
mouth; From the produce of his lips he shall be filled.
Death and life are in the power of the tongue,
and those who love it will eat its fruit.

PROVERBS 18:20,21

Whether you realize it or not, you are eating your words. The fruit of negative words produce a negative life, while the fruit of positive words produce a positive life.

Because of Jesus' death, burial, and resurrection, He regained dominion over the devil that Adam and Eve's sin had relinquished. Jesus then gave that dominion back to believers. The way we exercise our dominion is by speaking the words that God gives us to speak—words that are in agreement with His Word.

God planned for you and me to be in the earth at this time. He has a job for each of us to do. To get that job done, we must cooperate with His way of getting His will

68

accomplished in the earth, and His way is *through the words that we speak.*

God created the world with His words. Hebrews 11:3 says, *"By faith we understand that the worlds were framed by the word of God...."* Every part of creation came into being when God spoke.

Psalm 103:20 AMP says, *"Bless (affectionately, gratefully praise) the Lord, you His angels, you mighty ones who do His commandments, hearkening to the voice of His Word."* The angels are ready to move when you speak the Word of God. This is why I want to encourage you to personalize scriptures, then decree and declare them.

Always remember that *what is in your hand—the rod of God's Word—is going to swallow up what is in the enemy's hand.*

DECLARATION OF FAITH

I hunger and thirst daily after God's Word.
By the words of my lips, I am creating a positive,
successful life. I lift the rod of God's Word
and impossible situations become possible.

— 35 —

Your Words Will Direct Your Life

Pleasant words are like a honeycomb,
sweetness to the soul and health to the bones.

PROVERBS 16:24

Your words will either cause blessing or curses to come into your life. They will take you up or bring you down. You can change the atmosphere of your soul with pleasant words, such as: *In my pathway is life and there is no death. (Prov. 12:28.) The joy of the Lord is my strength. (Neh. 8:10.) Because You are my Shepherd, I shall not want. (Ps. 23:1.) You will never leave me or forsake me. (Heb. 13:5.)*

James 3:3-4 talks about how a bit is able to control a horse and how a small rudder is used to steer a large ship.

I remember as a little boy going to my grandfather's house. We later went to a dairy farm that had several Shetland ponies in the pasture. I was about eight or nine years old, and a boy that age can't just *look* at Shetland ponies without riding one of them!

I'll never forget jumping on that little pony and grabbing hold of its mane. There was no bit in its mouth. That was one of the worst rides I ever had because I couldn't control where the pony went. I was only able to get off the *hard* way. I fell off and hit the ground hard!

Some people's lives are like that. It's like they're on a runaway horse. Their lives are spinning out of control. Why? They aren't controlling their tongues.

If you get control of your tongue, you can direct your entire life the way it is supposed to go. Begin speaking the truth of God's Word, and you will see your life driven by the Word of God instead of the storms of life.

DECLARATION OF FAITH

I yield my tongue to the Lord, and I choose to speak what the Word says instead of what I see surrounding me. My tongue speaks life because Jesus' life is in me.

— 36 —

More Than Conquerors

*Yet in all these things we are more than
conquerors through Him who loved us.*

ROMANS 8:37

This is God's Word to you. "We" means you. Your position of being *"...more than a conqueror..."* is right now. The fact that you *are now* more than a conqueror is reality. It is the truth. Faith is always now, and your faith makes you a conqueror right now! It is something you are guaranteed because of God's promise.

To be a conqueror is tremendous. *Conquer* means "to triumph, to overcome, to win, to succeed, or to be victorious." Romans 8:37 in the *New American Standard Bible* is translated, *"...we overwhelmingly conquer through Him who loved us."* This is our victory! The adversary is defeated and can no longer triumph in our lives.

You are more than a conqueror because Jesus' love is in you, and His victory is yours by faith, not by works. No matter what you have done or how you may have failed in the past, you are *more than a conqueror*. Don't ever forget it.

See yourself standing up to the attacks of the enemy and overcoming all of them. The devil is defeated. Make this your daily confession of your victory and the devil's defeat.

You walk and live on the level of what you believe and say. Where you are today is a result of what you have believed and confessed yesterday.

Look into the Word of God to learn who you are in Christ. Then be so single-minded about who you are that nothing, no person, or no situation can ever change that image.

Accept your position as a conqueror. Your victory is guaranteed in Christ!

DECLARATION OF FAITH

*I am more than a conqueror, and I conquer ever
obstacle I face. Victory is a way of life for me
because Jesus won the victory for me.
Now He is winning victories through me.*

— 37 —

You Can Do All Things Through Christ

I can do all things through Christ who strengthens me.

PHILIPPIANS 4:13

You are unbeatable in Christ. There is nothing that God wants you to do that you cannot accomplish. It is through the strength of Jesus that you can meet any challenge.

Fear cannot stay when you realize that you can do all things through Christ. You don't have to be tormented anymore when you realize the source of your strength.

Paul could make this bold statement because Christ lived in him. Jesus lives in you as well, so you can say exactly the same thing. Your victory is not because of your education or ability; it's because Christ lives in you.

It is the truth of God's Word that sets you free. (John 8:32.) Acknowledge that Christ is in you and living His life

74

through you. Say this boldly every day: *I can do all things through Christ who strengthens me.*

When you realize who you are in Christ and what you can do through Him, you will never again be stopped from beginning a new Spirit-led project. In the past, you may have hesitated because you didn't know how to begin or what to expect. The unknown brought fear and ultimately paralyzed your expansion and growth. But now you can do all things through Christ.

If someone is in need of counseling, or your church needs a Sunday school teacher, or an unsaved family member needs an intercessor, you *can* do the job. Never again say the words, "I can't." Christ's ability resides in you, and you can do anything!

DECLARATION OF FAITH

I can do anything God wants me to do.
I am available to serve in the kingdom of God.
I can witness with power. I can win souls for Jesus.
I can love with Jesus' love. I can go the second mile.
I can pray without ceasing. I can rejoice at all times.

— 38 —

Receive the Promise

Grace and peace be multiplied to you in the
knowledge of God and Jesus our Lord,
As His divine power has given to us all things that
pertain to life and godliness, through the knowledge
of Him who called us by glory and virtue,
By which have been given to us exceedingly great and
precious promises, that through these you may be
partakers of the divine nature, having escaped the
corruption that is in the world through lust.

2 PETER 1:2-4

God has provided many promises in His Word that you can believe and receive, or stand on, in your own life. To partake of these promises is to partake of the life of God.

God's Word is unshakeable, unchangeable, unstoppable, and unending. Living by the Word is two-sided: 1) obeying God's commands; and 2) believing His promises.

When we meet God's conditions, His promises are released into our lives.

Hebrews 6:12 says that we inherit the promises of God through *faith* and *patience*.

Years ago, a young man in our youth group, a great runner at Hale High School in Tulsa, Oklahoma, developed cancer in his leg. The medical diagnosis was that his leg would have to be amputated. The scriptural promise from Proverbs 3:26 KJV was shared with him: *"For the Lord shall be thy confidence, and shall keep thy foot from being taken."* This young man caught a hold of the Word and believed God's promise. The following day, prior to surgery, he and his family asked his doctor to reexamine his leg. When the doctor checked his leg again, he couldn't find any cancer. Today, the young man still has his leg.

You must know the promises of God, believe them, and apply them to have victory in your life.

DECLARATION OF FAITH

I am a promise hunter. God has given me everything that pertains to life and godliness. Through faith and patience, I possess the promises of God.

— 39 —

Becoming a Champion for God

[Jesus said,] ...whoever desires to become
great among you shall be your servant.
And whoever of you desires to be first shall be slave of all.
For even the Son of Man did not come to be served,
but to serve, and to give His life a ransom for many.

MARK 10:43-45

You can be a champion for the Lord. It's not how many home runs you hit, how beautiful you are, how much real estate you own, or any other success there is. Becoming a champion for God is what you do for Him. The key to becoming a champion is being a servant.

Years ago, we joined forces with Feed the Children, the Power Team, and the Convoy of Hope to have a feeding outreach and to preach the gospel.

We were praying when the first people who came for food arrived an hour early—a grandma in a wheelchair with six kids. She said, "I need a little help." One of her daughters had been killed in an accident, another daughter was in prison, and she was raising their children. What a joy it was to give her some food. A servant of the Lord had driven her and the children to our site to get some food. Both the grandma and the woman who drove her were champions.

The stairway to championship is servanthood. Sometimes servants are not known by anyone on earth, but they are known by our Father in heaven.

DECLARATION OF FAITH

To walk in victory is to become like Jesus who made
Himself of no reputation and took on
the form of a bondservant. (Phil. 2:7.)
Self-service in my life stops today. I am motivated
by God's love to serve others in every way I can.

— 40 —

A Snapshot of Healing

...I will hasten my word to perform it.

JEREMIAH 1:12 KJV

God will honor your faith—what you are believing and speaking. As you find promises in God's Word for what you need, pray these promises and expect miracles.

Stay "promise-focused" by meditating on God's Word. God *will* do what He said in His Word. God sent His Word to accomplish His will and to bring His ways and His thoughts to the earth.

When our daughter Ruthie was a student at Oral Roberts University, she woke up one morning and one side of her face was paralyzed. She couldn't move it, and she couldn't speak plainly. We believe in doctors, medicine, hospitals, nurses, vitamins, and exercise—anything that contributes to healing and wholeness. We also believe in faith, miracles, prayer, and healing from God. We prayed with Ruthie and stood on the promises of God's Word, but we also sought medical help. Ruthie was diagnosed with Bell's Palsy. There was nothing the doctor's could do and no medicine to treat the condition.

At that time, Ruthie was our children's pastor. That week she was scheduled to teach on healing. She didn't back out. With severe symptoms still in her body that affected her appearance and speech, she taught on healing as strong as anyone possibly could. Later that week, her face straightened out.

I asked her, "How did your healing manifest?"

She said, "I stood on Hebrews 11:1: *Now faith is the substance of things hoped for, the evidence of things not seen.* My faith took a picture of healing before it was fully developed in my body!"

In the inner room of your heart, you can place faith images by believing the promises of God's Word. Ruthie's faith *spoke* the Word that she believed in her heart. Begin putting faith images in your heart by feeding on the promises of God's Word.

DECLARATION OF FAITH

The image of the Healer and His healing virtue, based on 1 Peter 2:24, is in my heart. I have victory in the area of healing because of the stripes Jesus bore on His back for my healing.

— 41 —

The Limitless Strength of God

He gives power to the weak, and to those
who have no might He increases strength.
Even the youths shall faint and be weary,
and the young men shall utterly fall,
But those who wait on the Lord shall renew their
strength; they shall mount up with wings like eagles, they
shall run and not be weary, they shall walk and not faint.

ISAIAH 40:29-31

It's time for you to soar with eagles and ride upon the high places of the earth. Isaiah was saying in these verses, "God never gets tired. He has unlimited strength and wisdom." In fact, strength is found in the wisdom of God. Weariness isn't necessarily tiredness of the body. The weariness most people experience is in their minds and attitudes. When a person becomes burdened, he carries "the load," which includes worry, fear, anxiety, and problems.

Perhaps you are in a place of weariness and fainting. You have thought about giving up on what God has called you to do. There is good news for you. God does not run out of strength. There is no end to His wisdom and under- standing. The good thing about God's strength and ability is that He wants to impart it into your life. He gives power to the faint because He intends for you to be powerful in the earth.

Born-again believers need to daily recharge their spir- itual reserves to face the difficulties, temptations, pres- sures, stress, demands, and schedules. If you try to be strong in the arm of your flesh, you will come to a point where you will want to give up on life.

Many people today who were once in church have gradually lost their communion and close fellowship with God. Their zeal for God has lessened to the point that the things of this world have become more attractive to them.

When you lose your desire for God, something else takes first place in your heart. As you draw close to the Lord, the things of this world will lose their power and influence over you. It is time to wait on the Lord, renew your strength, and mount up with wings as an eagle.

DECLARATION OF FAITH

I choose to be zealous for God.
The things of this world are not attractive to me.
I choose to wait upon the Lord.
I will not grow weary or faint.
I will soar with eagles and ride upon the high places
of the earth because I spend time waiting on the Lord.

— 42 —

Ask What You Will

"If you abide in Me, and My words abide in you, you will ask what you desire, and it shall be done for you."

JOHN 15:7

God has invited you to ask Him anything and watch it be granted for you. What a way to live! God's Word is a joy and delight. God says if you live in the Word and the Word lives in you, everything you ask will be granted.

To abide in Jesus is to remain in fellowship and communion with Him. What a privilege to have conversations with Him every day.

The Word abides in us as we allow it to dwell in our hearts and minds. Meditation of the Word is a key to getting it in your heart. Read it, study it, and hear what God is saying to you. Speak it, and mutter it to yourself. Think about it, and imagine yourself doing the Word.

Ask what you will, and it shall be done. If you are fellowshipping with the Lord in prayer and allowing His Word to dwell in you, then you will only desire God's will.

God has given you a special position as His child. What you ask shall come to pass. It shall be answered. God is willing to fulfill your desires. He wants you to have whatever you want when you are surrendered to Him.

Traditional thinking has been contrary to this truth. The idea has been put forth that our will is so opposite to God's will that everything we would desire is wrong. When you were born again, He put His Spirit in you. As you renew your mind with His Word, His thoughts become yours.

The truth is, God wants you to have more and enjoy more than you ever dreamed. The power to see your dreams come true is through fellowshipping with the Father and dwelling in the Word. Receiving what you ask becomes secondary to the joy of your time in the Word and prayer.

DECLARATION OF FAITH

The Word abides in me; therefore, everything
I ask for shall be given to me. God's desires are being
implanted in my heart as I fellowship with Him
and those desires are fulfilled by my Father.

— 43 —

Blessed With Every Spiritual Blessing

Blessed be the God and Father of our Lord Jesus Christ,
who has blessed us with every spiritual
blessing in the heavenly places in Christ.

EPHESIANS 1:3

We give thanks and praise to God for blessing us abundantly. He has *already* blessed us with every spiritual blessing in the heavenly places in Christ. All we will ever need has already been provided through Jesus.

Everything that we see in the world is a product of the unseen world of the Spirit. God is a Spirit. He spoke the world into existence using His faith. The unseen God created a visible world. Therefore, the world is a product of the spiritual, or the unseen. Understanding this is important in understanding your spiritual blessings in heavenly places.

The fact that you are blessed with spiritual blessings does not mean that there aren't any provisions for natural needs. Every natural provision is stored for you as a spiritual blessing in heavenly places. It comes forth into a visible, tangible provision as you use your faith. The same principle God used in bringing natural provisions into the earth from the unseen world of the Spirit is the same principle you can use to get your needs met, and that is faith.

Since your blessings are kept in heavenly places in Christ, they cannot be stolen, corrupted, or destroyed. Inflation or natural disaster never affects the godly person who has his treasure stored in heaven.

You are blessed because God has already given you everything you will ever need. Knowing and believing this, you don't have to fear lack in any area. The bank of heaven is full and secure. Its windows are open to you.

DECLARATION OF FAITH

I am a blessed person. Everything I need is found in Jesus.
Blessings from God have overtaken my life.
Goodness and mercy follow me everywhere I go.
Every day, God's blessings overflow in my life. My every
need is supplied according to God's riches in glory.

— 44 —

A New Creation

Therefore, if anyone is in Christ,
he is a new creation; old things have passed away;
behold, all things have become new.

2 CORINTHIANS 5:17

You are a brand-new species. You have received a new nature since you came to Jesus Christ. God's life—His eternal life—is now in you. Your spirit has been recreated to be like God.

To be in Christ means that you are born again. The new birth happens by faith—it is a gift from God. You cannot earn it or merit it. Salvation is God's free gift. The moment you confess Christ and believe on Him, you become brand new. You begin as a new baby in the kingdom of God. You are a new child in the family of God.

Everything in your life is new. Begin to believe it and say it aloud: *My entire life is new in Jesus. All things* means "all things." Everything is new. Accept this miracle. Your attitudes, desires, goals, thoughts, and concepts are new because of the life of God that now dwells in you.

All of the old junk that was associated with your old life has passed away. Its power and rule over your life have ended. Fear, addiction, hate, lust, envy, depression, and confusion all are part of the world system. The moment you become a new creation, these things no longer have a right to be a part of you.

Declare your liberty; accept the freedom that Jesus has given you. It is through faith in your heart and confession of your mouth that causes God's wonderful blessings to be apparent in your life.

Just because you do not see all the old things leave immediately, there is no reason to quit confessing 2 Corinthians 5:17. Faith is taking God at His Word and acting on it as truth.

DECLARATION OF FAITH

I am a new creation. All of the old things of my unsaved life have passed away. All things have now become new in me. I am a new person and God's life dwells in me. I am made a new creation in the image of God.

— 45 —

Prosper and Be in Health

*Beloved, I pray that you may prosper in all things
and be in health, just as your soul prospers.*

3 JOHN 2

God's will for you is prosperity and health in every area of your life. He is healthy. There is no sickness found in Him, and He desires His children to live in health. He wants you to have a healthy spirit, soul, and body.

The Apostle John wrote this verse by inspiration of the Holy Spirit and revealed God's will for every believer. God is no respecter of persons. (Acts 10:34.) His will expressed to the Christians to whom John wrote is still His will for you.

The phrase *"...I pray..."* could be translated "I will," "I wish," or "I desire." God really wants you prosperous and healthy. *"...In all things..."* indicates that God has placed these blessings as His top priority.

Godly prosperity and health begin on the inside of your soul. Notice the phrase *"…as your soul prospers."* The outward, external health and prosperity seen by others is only an expression of a far greater health and prosperity inside of you.

As you grow in mercy, love, gentleness, kindness, and goodness, your physical circumstances will be affected. People will want to know the God you serve because they will see in you the prosperity and health He gives. Your life is the most effective billboard the kingdom of God has. Let your light shine. Think it. Talk it. Live it! God's will is health and prosperity for the total man.

God's prosperity is always evidenced by generosity and humility. There isn't any room for stinginess or haughtiness when God's love has filled your heart. For it is His love that has prospered you and made you whole.

DECLARATION OF FAITH

I am healthy and prosperous in my spirit, soul, and body.
God's Word is planted deep in my heart. The Word
of God has transformed my soul. As I prosper inside
my spirit being, my outer man is also prospering.

— 46 —

God Is for You

...If God is for us, who can be against us?...Who shall bring a charge against God's elect? It is God who justifies.

ROMANS 8:31,33

God is for you. He goes before you and stands beside you. He is your rearguard. He surrounds you with His love and protection. He has taken up your cause since you joined yourself to Him.

This scripture makes us invincible. You are unbeatable, for there is no foe who is a match for God. Who can rise up against God Almighty and win?

God said, *"'I will never leave you nor forsake you.' So we may boldly say: 'The Lord is my helper; I will not fear. What can man do to me?'"* (Heb. 13:5,6).

God has promised to never abandon you in a tight spot. He doesn't get nervous when the situation is pressing. You see, the God of Israel neither slumbers nor sleeps. (Ps. 121:4.) He is always available.

From here on, don't allow yourself to be upset by adverse circumstances. Since God is for you, circumstances are no longer a factor. God holds the deciding vote, and good news: He has voted in your favor!

Situations no longer have to determine your decisions. Instead, listen to God. He will tell you what to do. The situation—whatever it may be—has to change and line up with the Word.

DECLARATION OF FAITH

God is for me. There is no opposition that can stop me. There is no force that can stand against me. I achieve everything God has called me to do. It is God who makes me a winner. He dominates the enemy through me. Jesus is living big inside me. I am never alone. Fear is a thing of the past, and winning is my new way of life.

— 47 —

Guidance From the Lord

The steps of a good man are ordered by the Lord,
and He delights in his way.

PSALM 37:23

God wants to order, guide, and direct your steps. A real key to receiving daily guidance from the Lord is to *acknowledge Him* as Proverbs 3:5-6 states: *"Trust in the Lord with all your heart, and lean not on your own understanding; in all your ways acknowledge Him, and He shall direct your paths."*

As a born-again believer, Christ lives on the inside of you. You can ignore Him or acknowledge Him. To acknowledge Him in all your ways is to recognize that Jesus has the wisdom, insight, guidance, and direction that you need. He promises to show you what to do and the direction to take when you lean on Him instead of trying to figure things out on your own.

Years ago when Sharon and I were traveling in ministry, we were on the interstate driving through

Houston. I saw an exit sign and the Lord spoke to me, "Turn off." I had to cross several lanes to do so, but we got off the interstate. Sharon asked me, "What are we doing?" I said, "I don't know, but the Lord said to turn off here."

We stopped at the Galleria Mall; and as we walked through the entrance, we saw a high school friend who was in Houston, getting treatment for cancer at the M. D. Anderson Hospital. Because our steps were ordered by the Lord, we were able to share the Word of healing with him. We laid hands on him and prayed for him. Afterward, we left the mall, walked to our car, and got back on the interstate.

God wants to direct your steps in that same way. He is arranging divine encounters for you not only to bless you but so you can be a blessing to others as well.

DECLARATION OF FAITH

My steps are ordered, guided, directed, and established by the Lord. I am always in the right place at the right time. He delights in leading me into victory in every area of my life.

— 48 —

All Things Work Together for Good

And we know that all things work together
for good to those who love God, to those
who are the called according to His purpose.

ROMANS 8:28

You are called according to God's purpose, which is first of all to be redeemed. God called and you accepted His redemption plan. Don't question that calling. Verbally affirm, *I am called according to God's purpose.*

We *know* that all things are working together for your good. This is not a hopeful wish. There is no guessing when it comes to the promises of God. We can know without a doubt or question because God is not a man that He would lie. (Num. 23:19.)

This means that any and all adversity *will* turn around. As you stand in faith and speak the Word, those situations will begin to line up in your favor.

I want to encourage you to also get your faith out for future circumstances. Too many people wait until something bad happens before they claim this promise. They look back and say, "Well, it will all work out for good." How about starting *now* and believing this for your future?

Sometimes circumstances appear to be working out differently than what you had planned. If this is the case, don't drop your confession. Many times God has something better for you than what you thought possible. Regardless of what you see happening, continue to boldly proclaim, *All things are working together for good in my life.*

Many unexpected blessings are coming your way. Breakthrough is just around the corner when you release faith in this portion of the Word.

DECLARATION OF FAITH

All things are working together for good in my life.
Everything is fitting into God's perfect plan.
I am called according to God's purpose, and
I will fulfill His plan and purpose in my life.

— 49 —

Stepping Stones or Stumbling Blocks?

*Fear not, for I am with you; be not dismayed, for I am
your God. I will strengthen you, yes, I will help you,
I will uphold you with My righteous right hand.*

ISAIAH 41:10

B y an act of your own will, you can let God turn your
scars into stars. Stumbling blocks can be turned into
stepping stones. God can turn the bad things that
have happened to you into something that will work for
your good.

Sometimes bad things happen because of our own
mistakes, faults, or sins. Sometimes they happen because of
the mistakes of others—their shortcomings, sins, and failures. On the other hand, bad things can also happen when
we are doing something good.

In these instances, an attack, or an assault from the
enemy, is used to distract you from doing the will of God.

Paul said, "...*all who desire to live godly in Christ Jesus will suffer persecution*" (2 Tim. 3:12).

If you set your sails to go against the enemy, you will encounter opposition and persecution for living in a godly manner. Do not become discouraged. God said that He will be with you, He will strengthen you, and He will uphold you with His right hand. (Isa. 41:10.)

In the lives of both Jesus and the Apostle Paul, people didn't exactly stand up and cheer when the sick were healed and devils were cast out. While some *were* happy, others were greatly disturbed and angry at what was happening. Stephen was stoned to death, and James was beheaded. Paul was persecuted constantly—not for doing wrong, but for doing right.

The good news for us is what Jesus accomplished on the Cross. He said in John 16:33: "...*In the world you will have tribulation; but be of good cheer, I have overcome the world.*" Because Jesus has overcome the world, we need to see ourselves from His perspective—seated in heavenly places with Him. (Eph. 2:6.) We are overcomers!

DECLARATION OF FAITH

God is turning my scars into stars.
I see myself seated in heavenly places with Christ Jesus.
I will overcome tribulation, tests, trials, and
persecutions because the Overcomer lives in me.

— 50 —

Freely Given All Things

He who did not spare His own Son, but delivered
Him up for us all, how shall He not
with Him also freely give us all things?

ROMANS 8:32

You have been given God's greatest gift—His Son, Jesus Christ. The fullness of God dwells in the Lord Jesus Christ. When you asked Jesus to come into your heart, the fullness of God now dwells in you. Think about this. If God did not withhold the best He had from you, why would He withhold anything of lesser value?

Everything you will ever need is yours *now*. There are no limits on the things God will give His children who love Him and put their faith in Him.

Since Jesus is your Shepherd, you never need to want or lack again. You have an abundant God who is willing to give you the very best He has and anything that you need. Expect this.

The children of Israel are examples of God's commitment to His people. God supplied whatever they needed. Deliverance from bondage came when they cried unto Him. He crushed their enemies in the Red Sea when they had nowhere to turn. God provided food, water, warmth, protection, and guidance to them while they wandered in the desert. He was their everything.

God has never changed. He is the same yesterday, today, and forever. (Heb. 13:8.) Through Jesus Christ, we have an open supply line between heaven's storehouse and us.

DECLARATION OF FAITH

God delivered up His Son for me. Through Jesus,
the Father freely gives me all things to enjoy.
I am able to share freely with others because
I know I have an abundance to give. My days of
lack are over. The time of abundance has come.
My Father is El Shaddai—the God who is
more than enough. Jesus has provided
all the things I will ever need.

— 51 —

Exceedingly Abundantly Above

Now to Him who is able to do exceedingly
abundantly above all that we ask or think,
according to the power that works in us.

EPHESIANS 3:20

G od's ability to work on your behalf is unlimited.
The Amplified Bible translation of this verse
says God "...*is able to [carry out His purpose and] do*
superabundantly, far over and above all that we [dare] ask or
think [infinitely beyond our highest prayers, desires, thoughts,
hopes, or dreams]."

Just imagine the highest, the richest, and the best
that the world has to offer. God is able to do superabundantly, far above anything you can imagine. The important
thing to know is that He *wants* to do this for you. God
desires far more for you than you could ever dream.

You get what you expect. Make it a practice to ask God for the greatest and the highest of all your desires. Then acknowledge that you expect exceedingly abundantly above what you have asked.

Usually the vision of a normal person is far below God's ability to bless him or her. If that is you, ask God to expand your vision and increase your level of expectancy.

There are no limitations with God. He knows no boundaries. What is impossible with man is always possible with God. (Luke 18:27.)

The fact that God wants to do exceedingly abundantly above all we ask or think does not make it automatic. You must believe and receive by faith. Stand on this promise for the superabundant blessings of God—they belong to you. Don't settle for barely getting along or just enough. God wants you to have exceedingly abundantly above that.

DECLARATION OF FAITH

I believe God is doing superabundantly above all I ask,
hope, dream, or desire in every area of my life.
I expect God's blessings to come on me continually.

— 52 —

Taking Your Jerichos

By faith the walls of Jericho fell down after
they were encircled for seven days.

HEBREWS 11:30

Jericho was a walled city that kept the children of Israel from marching into the Promised Land. Today, there are Jerichos that stand between you and your promised land of blessing. If you don't take Jericho, or the obstacle that faces you, you will never receive the blessing God has for you.

There are walled cities that come against homes and families. Sickness and disease, financial lack, and oppression are just a few examples.

Second Corinthians 10:4-5 says, *"For the weapons of our warfare are not carnal but mighty in God for pulling down strongholds, casting down arguments and every high thing that exalts itself against the knowledge of God, bringing every thought into captivity to the obedience of Christ."*

In the same way that Jericho fell in Joshua 6, your Jerichos will fall by faith today. If you are going to take your

Jerichos, you can't be a whiner, a complainer, or weak. You have to *"be strong and very courageous..."* just as God commanded Joshua. (Josh. 1:7.)

If the Word of God is not in your mouth, you can march around all the cities you want, and they will not fall. Like Joshua, let the power of God flow through you by believing and speaking the anointed Word of God.

When I was praying about whether or not we should start Victory Christian Center, I was scheduled to go on a trip to Israel. I didn't really want to go because I had not heard from the Lord on what I should do about starting the church. Since I had made a commitment to go, I went. One day I was praying on the shores of Galilee for direction, and God gave me three words: *Go for it!* We obeyed God and the church exploded in growth.

To take your Jerichos, *obey God's commands explicitly. Do not open your mouth in unbelief. Be sensitive to God's timing, and be diligent, courageous, and persevering!*

DECLARATION OF FAITH

*The power of God's anointed Word flows from
my lips just as it did from Joshua's lips.
I am not intimidated by the Jerichos I face.
As I obey the Lord, they are removed. I live in victory!*

— 53 —

Take Back What the Enemy Has Stolen

Now there were four leprous men at the entrance
of the gate; and they said to one another,
"Why are we sitting here until we die?
"If we say, 'We will enter the city,' the famine is in the
city, and we shall die there. And if we sit here, we die
also. Now therefore, come, let us surrender to the army
of the Syrians. If they keep us alive, we shall live;
and if they kill us, we shall only die."

2 KINGS 7:3,4

The four leprous men knew they were going to die if they didn't get something to eat. In contemplating their plight, they made the unlikely decision to go to the enemy's camp. As they went, God made their feet sound like an entire army and the Syrians fled in fear, leaving all of their food, supplies, and livestock behind.

The four leprous men entered the enemy camp and *"...went into one tent and ate and drank, and carried from it silver and gold and clothing, and went and hid them; then they came back and entered another tent, and carried some from there also, and went and hid it"* (2 Kings 7:8).

In the same way that these lepers marched directly into the enemy's camp, it's time for you to march toward your enemy and take back what the devil has stolen, the things that rightfully belong to you. It is God's will for you to be free in your spirit, soul, body, family, and finances. It is His will for you to own your own home debt free. It is God's will that you have a vehicle that runs well and is paid for. It is God's will for you to be out of debt and that you are in a position to be a blessing wherever you go. He wants you to live in absolute victory!

DECLARATION OF FAITH

Victory in my life includes freedom from debt.
I also have God's wisdom regarding financial stewardship.
I believe I will receive a seven-fold return on everything
the devil has stolen from me. (Prov. 6:30,31.)

— 54 —

Receiving an Overflow of God's Abundance

The thief comes only in order to steal and kill and
destroy. I came that they may have and enjoy life, and
have it in abundance (to the full, till it overflows).

An overflow of God's abundant provision for every area of your life is coming. I am challenging you to think higher, larger, and bigger than you have ever thought before concerning God's abundance. There is no bottom to His barrel of blessing.

There are people who have desired to put their children in a Christian school. To some, it's only a wish because there doesn't seem to be a way financially. Others have stepped into God's supernatural supply.

I think of Carmen Gil, our Hispanic pastor, a single mom who believed God to provide a way to enroll all three

110

of her children in our Christian school. God made a way for her. As you believe, He'll make a way for you too.

Things you never thought possible will happen in the days ahead. Expand your thinking and break out of the box that holds you back. You are not limited by the government or the company where you work. God's resources go beyond anything you can see in the natural.

Psalm 23:5 says, *"You prepare a table before me in the presence of my enemies; you anoint my head with oil; my cup runs over."*

The time for overflow is now. In addition to finances, this includes an overflow of joy, peace, and the opportunity to share with others what God has done for you.

DECLARATION OF FAITH

Because God is a God of overflow, my cup runs over.
God wants me blessed so I can be a blessing to others.
I receive abundant life in Jesus.

— 55 —

With Signs Following

And He said to them, "Go into all the world and preach
the gospel to every creature." And they went out and
preached everywhere, the Lord working with them and
confirming the word through the accompanying signs.

MARK 16:15, 20

Before Jesus ascended into heaven, He commanded
His disciples to preach the gospel to everybody in
the earth. The disciples were told to baptize those
who would believe. He guaranteed that signs would follow:
Devils would be cast out, believers would speak with new
tongues, no demon or deadly thing would harm them, and
they would lay their hands on the sick so they would be
healed. (v. 17.)

The disciples were obedient to Jesus' command. Signs
followed and thousands were freed as these bold believers
took Jesus at His Word. As they stepped out in faith, the
Spirit of God gave them power. They spoke the Word of
God in the name of Jesus and saw the miraculous happen.

It is no different today for you. You too are a disciple, a dedicated student and follower of the Lord Jesus Christ. You too are anointed by God's Spirit. You also have the command to tell the Good News and expect the signs to follow. The name of Jesus is still the same today as it was 2,000 years ago.

Proven principles will produce the same results any time they are followed. When you do what Jesus instructed, you too will see signs following. God is committed to confirming His Word. He doesn't confirm the doctrines of men or the philosophies of the world—He confirms His Word.

Rise up and let God fulfill His Word. You have been anointed to speak the Word with authority. God has brought you into the kingdom for such a time as this. (Est. 4:14.) Don't be afraid or embarrassed. Be bold and proclaim the gospel!

DECLARATION OF FAITH

I preach the gospel with authority. In the name of Jesus, the sick are healed and demons are cast out. The Word goes forth with power, and it is confirmed with signs following.

— 56 —

When Only a Miracle Will Do

Now a certain woman had a flow
of blood for twelve years,
And had suffered many things from
many physicians. She had spent all that she
had and was no better, but rather grew worse.
When she heard about Jesus, she came behind
Him in the crowd and touched His garment.
For she said, "If only I may touch
His clothes, I shall be made well."
Immediately the fountain of her blood was dried up, and
she felt in her body that she was healed of the affliction.

MARK 5:25-29

This woman had spent all her money on doctors; but instead of getting better, her condition grew worse. She was at the point of death when she *"heard about Jesus...."* She heard that He was healing the sick, and His message of healing got inside of her. "If He is healing others, He can heal me." She heard, she came, she spoke, and then she laid hold of Jesus' clothes.

As Jesus walked through the crowd, this woman connected with Him. Mark 5:30 says, *"And Jesus, immediately knowing in Himself that power had gone out of Him, turned around in the crowd and said, 'Who touched My clothes?'"* The woman *"...fell down before Him and told Him the whole truth"* (v. 33). In verse 34, Jesus spoke to the woman, *"...Daughter, your faith has made you well. Go in peace, and be healed of your affliction."*

When you have exhausted every avenue to meet your need and it looks as though there is no other way, whether it is healing, provision, or something else, Jesus is always available and accessible. You "connect" with Him by calling on His name. You lay hold of the promises of His Word through faith and by speaking them aloud. When nothing else will do, a miracle is waiting for you!

DECLARATION OF FAITH

Jesus is alive and is still performing miracles.
The fire and power of the Holy Spirit are flowing
through me. It is in Him that my seemingly impossible
situations are turned into great victories.

— 57 —

Delivered From the Devil's Traps

Surely He shall deliver you from the snare of
the fowler and from the perilous pestilence.
He shall cover you with His feathers, and
under His wings you shall take refuge;
His truth shall be your shield and buckler.

PSALM 91:3,4

Years ago Sharon was in a store with our little girls. She had them in a stroller. She got on an elevator with the girls and a man followed her on the elevator. A strange feeling suddenly came over Sharon.

Although the elevator had been operating, when the man pushed the numbers for different floors, the elevator door wouldn't close. He kept punching buttons but nothing happened. Finally, the man looked around and took off running. The moment he got out of the elevator, the elevator door shut and operated normally. Sharon later learned

116

from the building's security guard that he caught this man in a women's restroom.

Picture in your mind a giant eagle covering you with its wings as a shield of safety. That's the provision God has provided for your protection.

Ephesians 6:16 says that with the shield of faith *"...you will be able to quench all the fiery darts of the wicked one."* It's not God's will that any fiery dart of the devil touch your life.

DECLARATION OF FAITH

The Lord is my shield and buckler.
He delivers me from all of the devil's traps.
I will not fear evil for the Lord is with me.

— 58 —

God Originated the "Starting Over" Principle

While the earth remains, seedtime and
harvest, cold and heat, winter and
summer, and day and night shall not cease.

GENESIS 8:22

G od is the one who introduced the principle of a
"new start." In Genesis 1, He worked six days; and
on the seventh day, He rested. Sunday is the first
day of a new week. We praise God as we celebrate on
Sundays because it's resurrection day. Jesus arose on this
day, and the early church began to worship on the first day
of the week.

We celebrate a new day every day because the earth
rotates every twenty-four hours. No matter how dark it gets
in the night, morning always comes. A new moon comes up
monthly. Every year, we have a new beginning as the earth
makes one complete revolution around the sun. Then it
starts all over again.

After winter, comes spring. God said, *"While the earth remains, seedtime and harvest, cold and heat, winter and summer, and day and night shall not cease"* (Gen. 8:22).

God established the principle of "starting over" in everything. If you have a bad crop one year, you can start over and plant a new crop the next year. Each year brings a new harvest.

The Bible is filled with accounts of people beginning again. God made a beautiful, perfect garden and put Adam and Eve in it. In spite of its perfectness, they fell. The moment they fell, God initiated a new beginning. He told Satan that the seed of the woman would crush his head. (Gen. 3:15.) God set in motion a new beginning for mankind.

When Jesus came, a new beginning came to the earth. Even time would eventually be recognized as B.C. and A.D. When Jesus came, time began again. That was no accident. Life begins, not at birth, but with the acceptance of Jesus Christ in your heart as your personal Lord and Savior. This is the ultimate starting over principle.

DECLARATION OF FAITH

I'm going to put the principle of a "new start" into my own life. I'm planting a new crop and expecting a new harvest. This is my time of a new beginning in God.

— 59 —

Forgetting Those Things Which Are Behind

Brethren, I do not count myself to have apprehended;
but one thing I do, forgetting those things
which are behind and reaching forward
to those things which are ahead,
I press toward the goal for the prize of the
upward call of God in Christ Jesus.

PHILIPPIANS 3:13,14

The prize of the high calling of God is in Christ Jesus. Jesus is the prize or the reward that we seek. He's the purpose of your life, for in Him is life. Jesus said, "...*I am the resurrection and the life....*" (John 11:25).

When the Apostle Paul said, "...*I do not count myself to have apprehended...,*" he was saying, "I haven't arrived yet. I'm not perfect." He continued, "...*one thing I do, forgetting those things which are behind....*"

Do you have some things you'd like to forget from your past? It takes God's grace to forget. *Grace* is God's power, ability, and enablement. It's by His gift of grace that you are able to let go of the past, knowing that because of Jesus' shed blood, the past is wiped out.

People hold on to the past for several reasons. Some have experienced great things that have happened in the past, and in a nostalgic attitude, they relive them again and again.

Others hold on to a past that is filled with pain and regret. They play painful memories over and over again. Today is a great day to forget those painful memories and lay aside the things that keep you from moving forward.

If you are holding on to things of the past, it's impossible to receive the fresh and new. Paul let go of those things. He had some difficult years, as well as some great things to rejoice about. Yet, he said, "I'm forgetting the things that are behind me because there are greater things ahead of me."

Your future is going to be better than your past. You have everything to look forward to, because your future is out of this world.

DECLARATION OF FAITH

*I let go of the things of my past that are
holding me back from receiving God's best
for my life. I'm forgetting those things,
because greater things are ahead of me.
I am pressing for God's best in my life
and will live out my divine purpose.*

— 60 —

Reigning in Life

*For if by the one man's offense death reigned
through the one, much more those who receive
abundance of grace and of the gift of righteousness
will reign in life through the One, Jesus Christ.*

ROMANS 5:17

Adam's sin brought the entire human race into bondage. This verse says that death reigned by one, meaning the disobedience of Adam. Not only did mankind die physically, but it also died spiritually.

Sickness, disease, fear, torment, and poverty began to reign over the lives of people. Death became lord or master of the human race. Satan's power dominated the hearts and minds of the people on earth. As verse 17 says, *"death reigned."* Everything that is associated with death held the human race in bondage.

When Jesus died on the Cross, He destroyed the works of the devil. (1 John 3:8.) Today, the human race no longer needs to be under Satan's bondage. Jesus broke his reign of spiritual death.

"Inasmuch then as the children have partaken of flesh and blood, He Himself likewise shared in the same, that through death He might destroy him who had the power of death, that is, the devil, and release those who through fear of death were all their lifetime subject to bondage" (Heb. 2:14,15).

Follow this progression:

Satan—Sin—Death—Fear—Bondage

Now look at this progression:

Jesus—Righteousness—Life—Faith—Freedom

The moment you put your faith in Jesus, you receive eternal life, the righteousness of God, and freedom. You are no longer under the reign of death, but you now *"reign in life through the One, Jesus Christ."*

DECLARATION OF FAITH

I rule over circumstances and situations.
Sin, death, and fear have no hold over me for
I reign in life through Jesus Christ. Jesus' victory
over Satan has given me victory in every area of my life.

— 61 —

Kings and Priests

And from Jesus Christ, the faithful witness,
the firstborn from the dead, and the ruler over
the kings of the earth. To Him who loved us and
washed us from our sins in His own blood,
And has made us kings and priests to His God and
Father, to Him be glory and dominion forever and ever.
Amen.

REVELATION 1:5,6

You are loved by Jesus. He washed you from your sins in His own blood. No man will be cleaner than one who has been washed in the blood of Jesus. Soap and water only clean the body. The blood of Jesus cleans your soul. Your old life with its past sins is cleansed.

Jesus has made us kings and priests in His kingdom. And the kingdom of God is in us. We have been given authority to use Jesus' name to accomplish God's will in the earth.

You are an heir and a joint-heir with Jesus Christ. (Rom. 8:15,16.) Royal blood flows in your veins. As a result, you are a partaker of God's divine nature.

Furthermore, God has made you a priest. You are part of the kingdom of priests. As a priest, you are to go before God on behalf of men and go before men on behalf of God.

In the Old Testament, only certain men and women who were anointed as prophets, or prophetesses, and priests could contact God and hear from Him directly. However, in the New Covenant, every believer has received an anointing to serve as a priest. You do not need another person to go before God on your behalf. You can go directly to the Father through Jesus.

You are freed from all sin to live for God as His king and priest. Accept your office. Use your authority in prayer to bring God's will to pass in the earth. As you minister unto God, He will equip you to share with others.

DECLARATION OF FAITH

I am a king and a priest unto God. I have been
washed in the blood of Jesus. I walk in the
authority and in the anointing of God.

— 62 —

Heirs and Joint Heirs

*The Spirit Himself bears witness with
our spirit that we are children of God,
And if children, then heirs—heirs of God and
joint heirs with Christ, if indeed we suffer
with Him, that we may also be glorified together.*

ROMANS 8:16,17

Y ou have the Spirit of Christ living inside you. He is
the One who lets you know for certain that you
are a child of God. Since the Holy Spirit is living
inside of you, you don't have to experience doubts or
confusion anymore. You know that you know that you
know that you are a child of God.

As His child, you have become an heir of God. An
heir receives whatever is left to him in a will. Our will is
the New Testament. The Word says that a will or testament does not go into effect until the testator dies. Our
will (the New Testament) went into effect at the death of
Jesus Christ.

Not only did Jesus die that we might receive our inheritance, He also arose from the dead to be the executor of His own will. In other words, Jesus is the One who sees to it that we receive what was designated as ours in the will.

Everything that has been given to you in the New Testament is God's will for you. All of the promises and provisions mentioned are rightfully yours. You did nothing to earn or merit them—a rich relative just named you as an heir.

The blessing of being an heir of God expands with the phrase *"joint heirs with Christ."* Jesus, the Son of God, is heir to everything that the Father has. The Word calls you a joint heir or a co-heir with Jesus. Everything Jesus inherited as the Son of God is also part of your inheritance.

You have already been blessed far beyond anything you could imagine. Only God could have written such a marvelous will, with your name included in it. He has revealed God's will to you so you will know that you will never lack anything.

DECLARATION OF FAITH

Father, I thank You for loving me and including me in Your will. I am Your heir, and I am a joint heir with Jesus Christ. Today I choose to walk in the full inheritance of God.

— 63 —

Mountain Mover

So Jesus answered and said to them, "Have faith in God.
For assuredly, I say to you, whoever says to this
mountain, 'Be removed and be cast into the sea,' and
does not doubt in his heart, but believes that those things
he says will be done, he will have whatever he says."

MARK 11:22,23

You have the God-kind of faith. The moment you were born again, you received *"...a measure of faith"* (Rom. 12:3). In other places Jesus referred to faith as *"a mustard seed."* (Matt. 17:20.) The faith you have now is capable of moving any mountain in your life. The "God-kind" of faith resides in you now.

Jesus said, *"...Whoever says to this mountain...."* This means you are included since you are a "whoever." You can speak directly to the mountain and address it with authority. If the mountain is strife in the home or business, say, "Strife, in the name of Jesus, I command you to leave this place now." Then lift your hands and begin to thank God for removing the problem, or the mountain.

When you know your authority, you will believe that what you say *will* come to pass. You have this assurance because Jesus regained authority over the devil through His death and resurrection. (Matt. 28:18-20.) You expect your words to be fulfilled because of your covenant with God. Doubt has no place in you, for faith has flooded your heart.

You were born again to rule and reign in this earth under the authority of Jesus Christ. (Rom. 5:17.) Expect things to change as you speak, for God has given you the power to move mountains.

DECLARATION OF FAITH

I am a mountain mover. Jesus lives in me.
I have His nature, His name, His Word, His Spirit,
and His life. I believe in my heart that what I say
with my mouth comes to pass. I have what I say
because I am led by the Spirit. No obstacle can stand
against me. They are all removed in Jesus' name.

— 64 —

As He Is, So Are You

Love has been perfected among us in this:
that we may have boldness in the day of judgment;
because as He is, so are we in this world.

1 JOHN 4:17

The Word says you are as He is. You are made in the image of God. You are created in Jesus. You are identified with God by your nature for you have eternal life.

No longer do you need to fear when approaching God. You can go boldly before the throne of grace. (Heb. 4:16.) You can approach God without any fear of rejection. Although we don't see God with the natural eye, our spirit bears witness that we are His children. (Rom. 8:16.)

The people of this world fear the day of judgment. A sinner does not have peace about the day he or she dies. That is not so for the born-again Christian. Christians have the assurance that when we leave our bodies, we are in the presence of the Lord. (2 Cor. 5:8.)

God's love is perfected in you when you keep His Word. (1 John 2:5.) The Word reveals your right standing with God. There is a "right relatedness" or righteousness that belongs to every Christian. You are the righteousness of God (2 Cor. 5:21) for as He is, so are you. Jesus is righteous and everything He is, *you are*.

Think on this. When you asked Jesus into your heart, He now dwells in your spirit being. Since He is strong, you are strong. Make this your daily confession: *I am strong in the Lord and in the power of His might.* (Eph. 6:10.)

"But he who is joined to the Lord is one spirit with Him" (1 Cor. 6:17). You have the Spirit of God in you. You are a partaker of the nature of Jesus Christ—as He is, so are you.

As a young child, you might have been told, "Be like Jesus." Well, now you are like Him. You are a reflection of His glory and grace to those around you. Accept your God-given likeness: *"I am as He is."*

Faith is merely a matter of accepting the Word of God. If God says it, when you believe it, that settles it.

DECLARATION OF FAITH

Jesus is in me now, and I am as He is. I accept my position in Christ and reflect His glory and goodness to those around me.

— 65 —

Perfected

But may the God of all grace, who called us to His eternal glory by Christ Jesus, after you have suffered a while, perfect, establish, strengthen, and settle you.

1 PETER 5:10

Jesus has called you to eternal glory. Before He went to the Cross, He prayed that you would receive His glory. (John 17:22.)

You may be persecuted for your confession of Christ, but Jesus has already told you this would happen. He said, *"...In the world you will have tribulation..."* (John 16:33). Not everybody will rejoice when the sick are healed and devils are cast out. In essence, Jesus said not to be concerned about what others might say. *"...But be of good cheer, I have overcome the world"* (v. 33).

Since Jesus is an overcomer, you are also an overcomer by the power of the risen Christ in you.

You have the assurance that you are being perfected, established, strengthened, and settled. One version of the Bible says, *"…[God] will himself give you mastery, and steadiness, and strength"* (1 Peter 5:10 KNOX).

The Amplified Bible translates 1 Peter 5:10 as, *"…[God] will Himself complete and make you what you ought to be, establish and ground you securely, and strengthen, and settle you."*

You can say with the Psalmist David, *"The Lord will perfect that which concerns me…"* (Ps. 138:8). You are *"His workmanship, created in Christ Jesus for good works…"* (Eph. 2:10).

"And I am convinced and sure of this very thing, that He Who began a good work in you will continue until the day of Jesus Christ [right up to the time of His return], developing [that good work] and perfecting and bringing it to full completion in you" (Phil. 1:6 AMP).

DECLARATION OF FAITH

God is perfecting everything that concerns me.
I am His workmanship. I am complete in Jesus:
established, strengthened, and settled.
Thank You, Father, for perfecting me.

— 66 —

The Devil Touches
You Not

We know that whoever is born of God does not sin;
but he who has been born of God keeps himself,
and the wicked one does not touch him.

1 JOHN 5:18

You are born of God and the divine life of Jesus dwells in you. This holy presence of God's life in you is the power that will keep the wicked one from touching you.

God says that your righteousness is of Him. *"No weapon formed against you shall prosper..."* (Isa. 54:17).

You have been given a mighty shield of faith *"...with which you will be able to quench all the fiery darts of the wicked one"* (Eph. 6:16). *All* means "all." Whatever the devil tries to throw at you is destroyed by your shield of faith.

"Therefore submit to God. Resist the devil and he will flee from you" (James 4:7). Submitting to God means believing

and obeying the Word. When you do this and stand in faith, the devil has no choice but to leave.

First Peter 1:5 says that you *"...are kept by the power of God through faith...."* Believe this promise to you and act like it is so. In our battle against the devil, there is no room for fear or timidity.

The Word says the devil cannot touch you when you keep yourself. You keep yourself by walking in the love of God and being patient and full of faith.

Jesus gave you and every believer power over all the power of the enemy. (Luke 10:19.) You are commissioned to cast out devils. (Mark 16:17.)

Jesus defeated Satan on the Cross and stripped him of his power and authority. Don't allow yourself to worry about the devil. Say what the Word says about the situation.

DECLARATION OF FAITH

I am born of God. I keep myself and the wicked one
does not touch me. I resist the devil and he flees from me.
My shield of faith quenches every fiery dart.
The devil runs from me in terror. Demonic oppression
cannot touch me for I am kept by the power of God.

— 67 —

Favor

For You, O Lord, will bless the righteous;
with favor You will surround him as with a shield.

PSALM 5:12

F avor is like every other blessing and promise of God.
You receive favor from God and man to the degree
that you believe and accept this promise by faith.

Favor belongs to you. Abraham, Isaac, Jacob, Joseph,
Moses, Samuel, and Esther (to name a few Old Testament
leaders) all had supernatural favor. Favor is like resurrection
power. It keeps raising you up no matter what tries to put
you down. Favor is like a cork. When you put a cork under
water, it pops right back up to the top.

Potiphar's wife slandered Joseph and lied about him.
As a result, he was thrown in prison. Yet, in prison Joseph
had supernatural favor which caused him to be put in
charge of all of the inmates. While in prison, Joseph interpreted the dreams of a butler and a baker. The butler was
restored to his position, but the baker was hung, just as

Joseph had said. Joseph said to the butler, *"Remember me when it is well with you, and please show kindness to me; make mention of me to Pharaoh, and get me out of this house"* (Gen. 40:14).

The butler forgot Joseph until Pharaoh had a dream that no one could interpret. He then told Pharaoh what had happened to him in prison. Joseph was called, and he interpreted Pharaoh's dream. As a result, Joseph was promoted and set over all the land of Egypt. (Gen. 41:39-41.)

Favor has a purpose. God will bring you into favor so you can bring deliverance to people and help them. Once you receive Jesus Christ, you become a favored person. *"For whoever finds me finds life, and obtains favor from the Lord"* (Prov. 8:35).

DECLARATION OF FAITH

The supernatural favor that is upon my life enhances the work that God is doing through me. I am surrounded by favor as a shield.

— 68 —

Honor

*...Those who honor Me I will honor, and those
who despise Me shall be lightly esteemed.*

1 SAMUEL 2:30

G od wants to honor you, but if you refuse to honor
the things and people God honors, you will forfeit
the honor He wants to bring into your life—
respect, promotion, increase, and opportunities.

Galatians 6:7 says, *"Do not be deceived. God is not
mocked; for whatever a man sows, that he will also reap."* If you
sow honor into the lives of others, you will reap honor.

The movie *Chariots of Fire* was about a young man
from Scotland who ran in the 1924 Olympics in Paris. After
qualifying as the United Kingdom's representative for the
100-meter dash, he found out that this race was to be run
on Sunday. As a devout Christian, he refused to run on the
Lord's Day. He wanted his victory to be for the glory of
God. Since he was the fastest runner in the world at that

time, he would have won the Gold Medal. Great pressure was put upon him to run on Sunday, but he refused.

Another young man from the United Kingdom was to run a 400-meter race on another day. He had already won a Gold Medal, so he offered his spot in this race to Eric Liddell. Eric accepted, ran the 400-meter, and won the Gold Medal.

Before the race, a young Christian from America handed Eric a note. On it was scribbled, "1 Samuel 2:30, ...'Those who honor Me I will honor.'"

In 1981, *Chariots of Fire* won the Academy Award for Best Picture. The story of Eric Liddell was told all over the world. He was honored for his commitment to God. You, too, can honor God by refusing to compromise your commitment to Him.

DECLARATION OF FAITH

I am honoring the Lord by obeying His Word.
I am honoring those in positions of authority.
God's honor comes to me because of
the honor I have given Him.

— 69 —

Courage

By faith Moses, when he became of age, refused
to be called the son of Pharaoh's daughter,
Choosing rather to suffer affliction with the people of
God than to enjoy the passing pleasures of sin,
Esteeming the reproach of Christ greater riches than
the treasures in Egypt; for he looked to the reward.
By faith he forsook Egypt, not fearing the wrath of the
king; for he endured as seeing Him who is invisible.

HEBREWS 11:24-27

Courage will cause you to do what is right regardless of the consequences—to do what God says no matter what men say. It is standing up for God rather than compromising the truth. Moses is a great example of courage.

When our girls were small, Sharon saw a van of young people pull into a parking area across the street from our house. She felt led to go across the street and witness to them. Obviously, they were into drugs and partying. As she shared the Lord with them, they mocked her and made fun of her. She didn't allow their mockery to sway her from witnessing to them. One of the guys in the van said to the others, "Knock it off."

It takes courage to stand in the face of people who don't want to hear about Jesus, but Sharon stayed with it. She gave them my book *This New Life* and cards about our church. Finally, she was able to pray for them, but they wouldn't pray the sinner's prayer. She returned to our house and began to pray strongly for them.

Soon the doorbell rang. It was the guy who had told his buddies to "knock it off." He said, "I believe what you were saying," and apologized for the way one of the young men talked to her. Then he said, "I have a grandfather who believes like you, and I know he has been praying for me." Sharon said, "I know he is praying for you, or I wouldn't be in your pathway."

Be courageous for the things that count for eternity, and look for opportunities to share your faith with others.

DECLARATION OF FAITH

I choose to be courageous. I esteem the riches
of Christ greater than the pleasures of sin.
I will not fear the scorn of people but will
share the pathway of life with others.

— 70 —

Free Indeed

"Therefore if the Son makes you free,
you shall be free indeed."

JOHN 8:36

You have been set free by Christ. Jesus gained victory and freedom for you when He was raised from the dead. The moment you received Jesus, victory and freedom became yours.

Declare your independence! It is time to proclaim your emancipation. You have a bill of rights given to you by your heavenly Father through His Son, Jesus Christ. He has set you *"free indeed."* This means entirely, totally, completely, without any question, doubt, or objection. You are free!

You are free from the powers of Satan. You can say as Jesus said, *"...the ruler of this world is coming, and he has nothing in Me"* (John 14:30). Therefore, give no place to the devil. (Eph. 4:27.)

"Our soul has escaped as a bird from the snare of the fowlers; the snare is broken, and we have escaped. Our help is in the name of the Lord, who made heaven and earth" (Ps. 124:7,8).

The power of the enemy was broken when Jesus was raised from the dead. No snare of Satan, sin, or fear can hold you.

Not only are you free *fro m* the powers of darkness, you are also freed *into* the kingdom of light. You are free to love, give to others, enjoy the abundant life, and do acts of righteousness.

John 8:36 AMP reads, *"So if the Son liberates you [makes you free men], then you are really and unquestionably free."* Stand, therefore, in the freedom that Christ purchased for you.

DECLARATION OF FAITH

I will never again be enslaved by sin.
I am free from all the dominion of darkness.
Jesus has made me free in every area of my life.

— 71 —

God Will Vindicate You

For I am not ashamed of the gospel of Christ,
for it is the power of God to salvation for everyone
who believes, for the Jew first and also for the Greek.

ROMANS 1:16

I f you are not ashamed of the gospel, God will vindicate
you. If you will take a stand for what is right, for what
the Lord has told you to do, and obey His voice, your
day of vindication will come. To *vindicate* means "to clear of
suspicion, accusation, or doubt."

There are situations where people have done wrong.
I'm not speaking about failure or shortcomings. I am speaking about persecution against Christians simply because
they believe the truth about Jesus Christ.

There are many Bible examples of people being persecuted. Joseph, for example, was sold into slavery by his
brothers because of their jealousy of him. Joseph was
purchased by Potiphar and his wife later slandered him,

145

which resulted in his imprisonment, even though he was innocent of the charges.

That's not the end of the story. Even while Joseph was in prison, Scripture says, *"The keeper of the prison did not look into anything that was under Joseph's authority, because the Lord was with him; and whatever he did, the Lord made it prosper"* (Gen. 39:23).

The story does not end here either. God had given Joseph the ability to interpret dreams. When no one else in the land was able to interpret Pharaoh's dream, Joseph was called upon. He told Pharaoh the meaning of a dream and was catapulted from a lowly prisoner to the second in command of Egypt. *"And Pharaoh said to Joseph 'See, I have set you over all the land of Egypt'"* (Gen. 41:41).

What God did for Joseph, He will do for you as well. God doesn't have any favorites. If you will trust the Lord and obey His commands, regardless of persecution and opposition you experience, you will be vindicated.

DECLARATION OF FAITH

I will not grow weary in well doing, for in due season I will reap if I do not lose heart. (Gal. 6:9.) I trust God to vindicate me in the face of unjust accusations.

— 72 —

Overcomer

*"And they overcame him by the blood of the
Lamb and by the word of their testimony, and
they did not love their lives to the death."*

REVELATION 12:11

You have power over the devil and over the powers
of darkness. The blood of Jesus is the weapon that
you use against the attacks of the enemy. It will
stop him right in his tracks.

There is no reason to be intimidated by evil. As the
power of God fell on the day of Pentecost, releasing the
believers to boldly testify about Jesus, the Word says, *"Then
fear came upon every soul..."* (Acts 2:43). This scripture is
talking about the fear of God, or respect of what is holy.

God has given you two things in this scripture to
overcome the devil:

1.   The blood of the Lamb.

2.   The word of your testimony.

Satan is the accuser of the brethren. The blood of Jesus is your guarantee of God's mercy that gives you complete coverage on all your needs. The blood stops all accusations because it cleanses you from all sin. It is by faith that you are able to rise above any condemnation.

The word of your testimony is the confession of your faith in God's Word. It is the Word of God spoken out loud. It is acknowledging the Word of God as the truth for your life.

Regardless of what your circumstances look like, when you continually speak the Word, you will see your situation line up to the Word. Through the blood of Christ and the word of your testimony, you are victorious in every area of your life.

DECLARATION OF FAITH

I am a blood-bought overcomer. I am born of God.
I have God's nature, ability, and power to overcome
every obstacle I face. I cannot be defeated, for I continually
speak what the Word says and my situation changes.

Wise, Right, Clean, and Free

But of Him you are in Christ Jesus,
who became for us wisdom from God—and
righteousness and sanctification and redemption–
That, as it is written, "He who glories,
let him glory in the Lord."

1 CORINTHIANS 1:30,31

Our boasting, or our glory, is not in ourselves—it is in Christ Jesus. Jesus is wisdom. He is the righteousness of God. He is the sanctified one and the sanctifier. He is the redeemer and the redemption. Jesus is all in all. He is everything.

There is no room for you to boast in how wise you are. You can only boast in the wisdom of God. You see, everything that you are is yours by grace.

The Word says you are a new creation *"in Christ Jesus"* by virtue of the miracle of the new birth. (2 Cor. 5:17.) Not only are you *"in Christ,"* but Christ is also in you. (Col. 1:27.) The Holy Spirit lives inside you. You are the temple of the Holy Spirit. (1 Cor. 6:19,20.)

It is plain to see that Christ is in you and that you are in Christ. You have given your life to Jesus, because He has given His life for you.

God made Jesus to be your wisdom through the miraculous union that took place when you were saved. Jesus is your wisdom. He is your righteousness, your sanctification, and your redemption. These four things are found in Christ, and He is in you. Therefore, all of these things are in you.

DECLARATION OF FAITH

Jesus is my wisdom, my righteousness, and my sanctification.
I am redeemed. It's not by anything I have done, but what
Christ has done for me through His death on the Cross.
I do not boast in myself but only in the Lord.

— 74 —

Understanding

And He opened their understanding, that
they might comprehend the Scriptures.

LUKE 24:45

One of the greatest hindrances to progress and growth is lack of knowledge and understanding. God gives us understanding by His Spirit. (Job 32:8.) Understanding comes as revelation in the heart of man.

As two apostles walked on the road to Emmaus Jesus appeared to them, but they did not recognize Him. He began to explain the Scriptures to them. It was not until He opened their understanding that the truth came alive to them.

As you read the Word, it will be opened unto you as well, and you will have a complete understanding of what Christ has done for you.

If you have ever thought that God did not want you to know what He has in store for you, then you have thought wrong. First Corinthians 2:9 says, *"...Eye has not seen, nor ear heard, nor have entered into the heart of man the things which God has prepared for those who love Him."*

If we stopped right here and did not read the next verse, we could justifiably plead ignorance. However, the next verse changes everything.

"But God has revealed them to us through His Spirit. For the Spirit searches all things, yes, the deep things of God" (v. 10). God has given us revelation by His Spirit *"...that we might know the things that have been freely given to us by God"* (v. 12).

"Consider what I say, and may the Lord give you understanding in all things" (2 Tim. 2:7).

DECLARATION OF FAITH

*The Spirit guides me into all truth and enlightens the eyes of my understanding.
I have understanding of all things.
The Word is alive to me, and
I understand the deep things of God.*

— 75 —

Love Never Fails

Love never fails....

Love never disappears.... MOFFATT.

Love shall never pass away.... CONEYBEARE.

1 CORINTHIANS 13:8

You are born of love because you are born of God. (1 John 4:7.) The love of God has been shed abroad in your heart by the Holy Spirit. (Rom. 5:5.)

God is love. The very essence of God Himself has been poured into you. You cannot do anything in yourself to receive His love, for it is a gift that you receive.

God's love in you makes you victorious over hatred. When you harbor hate in your heart, it acts as a cancer and eats away at you. However, when the love of God is in your heart, you are immunized from the multiple diseases related to hate. Jealousy cannot grow when it comes in contact with the love of God.

God's power is wrapped up in His love. Love, therefore, becomes a limitless power source when you walk in it. When you choose to obey the law of love, you are acting in love.

When God's love is perfected in you, it casts out all fear. (1 John 4:18.) You know that God's love protects you at all times. It is ever on the alert. You need not be concerned that someone will offend you, because forgiveness is natural to you.

There is no fear in your life since nothing can separate you from the love of God. (Rom. 8:39.) God's love keeps on operating regardless of circumstances. Unlike city lighting systems, it cannot be knocked out by a bad storm. God's love prevails in adversity.

You have the capacity to love in all situations because God has put His love inside you. By confessing that you are a love person, you will strengthen the power of God's love in you.

DECLARATION OF FAITH

*I am born of love. God's love fills my life, and
I walk in love. Therefore, I am patient, kind, gentle,
longsuffering. Love in me never fails. Since love
does not fail, I do not fail. I forgive quickly for
I am a forgiver. Loving people is a way of life for me.*

The Battle Is Not Yours

And he said, "Listen, all you of Judah and you
inhabitants of Jerusalem, and you, King Jehoshaphat!
Thus says the Lord to you: 'Do not be afraid nor
dismayed because of this great multitude,
for the battle is not yours, but God's.'"

2 CHRONICLES 20:15

It is not entirely bad for a believer to face trouble—that is, if his trust is in God. *"The Lord is good, a stronghold in the day of trouble..."* (Nahum 1:7). When your trust is in God, it does not matter how much trouble rears its ugly head. God will deliver you.

The people of Judah were in trouble. The armies of Moab, Ammon, and Mount Seir had come against the land to destroy its inhabitants. It was a bleak time, but the people of God began to seek God through fasting and prayer. As the Spirit came upon Jahaziel, a Levite and a descendant of Asaph, he spoke these words: *"...The battle is not yours, but God's."*

The words the Holy Spirit spoke hundreds of years ago are just as true today. The battle is the Lord's. He has already fought and won the victory for every believer. Begin to rejoice, for you have heard from God.

As the children of Judah began to praise God, the Lord caused their enemies to fight one another. They stood and watched their enemies destroy themselves.

God's formula for success is still the same. Don't be afraid or dismayed when trouble appears. It is not your battle. God has committed Himself to fight on your behalf. He will contend with those who contend with you. (Isa. 49:25.)

DECLARATION OF FAITH

I am not afraid of any situation. I will not be dismayed at any time. These battles are not mine, but the Lord's. God fights all my battles. I am always victorious because God always wins. I refuse to worry about troubles or tribulations. Regardless of the circumstances, God always puts me over.

— 77 —

Stand Still—
See God's Salvation

"'You will not need to fight in this battle.
Position yourselves, stand still and see the salvation
of the Lord, who is with you, O Judah and Jerusalem!'
Do not fear or be dismayed; tomorrow go out
against them, for the Lord is with you."

2 CHRONICLES 20:17

After Judah had been surrounded by its enemies, they looked to God for help. His Word to them was, *"...the battle is not yours, but God's"* (v. 15). Hear this loud and clear: *Many battles are lost by Christians trying to fight battles by themselves.*

God delights in demonstrating His salvation in our lives. Accept it and rest in it. What He did for the Israelites was not His will for just one brief period in history. It is His will for all His people all the time.

If you face a situation that seems impossible, begin to rejoice. You're about to see the salvation of the Lord. Great faith is exercised by rest. Faith really is the easy way. It only looks hard from the natural man's viewpoint.

Take, for instance, the Roman centurion who Jesus said exercised great faith. All he asked Jesus to do was *"...speak the word only, and my servant shall be healed"* (Matt. 8:8 KJV). It was simple and easy. Jesus did the work, and the centurion believed. This is God's way for us to live.

Set yourself in faith in God's Word, and stand still. Realize that standing still sometimes requires more faith than moving about. Standing still indicates your trust is in God's ability and not your own. *"For we who have believed do enter that rest..."* (Heb. 4:3).

The rest of God is the life of faith. You will see the salvation of the Lord because you have set yourself to stand still.

DECLARATION OF FAITH

Whatever I do prospers and succeeds, for the Lord
fights all of my battles. I, therefore, live a life of rest.
The salvation of the Lord is ever before me,
and my enemies are destroyed before my eyes.
Circumstances change as I stand still before the Lord.

Sing and Praise to Victory

*"...Believe in the Lord your God, and you shall be
established; believe His prophets, and you shall
prosper."
And when he had consulted with the people,
he appointed those who should sing to the Lord,
and who should praise the beauty of holiness,
as they went out before the army and were saying:
"Praise the Lord, for His mercy endures forever."
Now when they began to sing and to praise,
the Lord set ambushes against the people
of Ammon, Moab, and Mount Seir, who had
come against Judah; and they were defeated.*

2 CHRONICLES 20:20-22

There is so much for you to receive from this great story. God's word to His people was, *"...The battle is not yours, but God's"* (v. 15). The people were instructed to *"...stand still and see the salvation of the Lord..."* (v. 17).

In the above verses, God instructs His people to believe His Word. In doing so, they will be established and prosper. Believing God is the key to prosperity and success. Salvation comes by believing God. Healing and the baptism of the Spirit both come by believing God. Believing God is the first step in receiving from God and seeing miracles.

God often gives us something to do as an expression of our faith in Him. In this case, He directed the people to begin to worship and praise Him for His mercy. Singers were designated to go out before the army and magnify God.

Singing praises to God is one of the highest expressions of faith. You can praise Him *before* you see any answer with your physical eyes. God's Word has already given you a clear picture of victory. It is yours *now*. Simply live the life of praise and worship. Let your life become a melody of praise.

DECLARATION OF FAITH

Father, I give You praise for my victory in You.
I rejoice in Your triumph over my enemies.
I thank You for the solutions to all the problems
I will ever face. Every day I will sing songs of
praise to You, Jesus. You are my everything.

— 79 —

There Is Liberty

...Where the Spirit of the Lord is, there is liberty.

2 CORINTHIANS 3:17

"The Spirit of the Lord is upon Me, because He has
anointed Me to preach the gospel to the poor;
He has sent Me to heal the brokenhearted,
to proclaim liberty to the captives and recovery of
sight to the blind, to set at liberty those who are
oppressed; to proclaim the acceptable year of the Lord."

LUKE 4:18,19

I t is through Jesus that you are healed, delivered, and set free. Liberty is yours now!

In relation to the Spirit of the Lord, Jesus said, *"...How much more will your heavenly Father give the Holy Spirit to those who ask Him!"* (Luke 11:13). If you have never received the Holy Spirit, ask and you shall receive.

The liberty the Spirit gives begins in the inner person. Your spirit is set free first of all to worship the Father.

Next, your soul is liberated to move in harmony with God's will. You no longer have to battle and *try* to obey God; you are free to serve Him with joy.

Your body is likewise set free by the Spirit of God. As you renew your mind to the Word and things of God, your spirit being dominates the dictates of your flesh.

This is life in the Spirit. It is liberty from poverty, sickness, fear, oppression, and sin. The Spirit is in you, and where the Spirit of the Lord is, there is liberty. You are liberated!

DECLARATION OF FAITH

I know the truth, and the truth has made me free.
The Spirit of the Lord has liberated me.
No fear can exist in me. Disease has no place in my body.
Sin has no dominion over me. The Spirit of the Lord has
liberated me in my spirit, soul, and body. I am free indeed!

— 80 —

You Have Overcome

Jesus said, "These things I have spoken to you,
that in Me you may have peace.
In the world you will have tribulation;
but be of good cheer, I have overcome the world."

JOHN 16:33

Jesus never deceived His disciples. He told them exactly
what they would face if they followed Him. He said,
"...You will have tribulation...." However, it is important to
note that Jesus did not dwell on that aspect. It was fact,
but He went on to say, *"...But be of good cheer, I have overcome*
the world."

In spite of what you may face, Jesus encourages you
to cheer up. Rejoice and be glad. Nothing you face will be
able to overcome Jesus. He said, *"...I have overcome the*
world." His death on the Cross was not for Himself alone. It
was for you. His victory is your victory!

Instead of living in fear and anxiety, you can now live
in faith and peace. Jesus said, *"...In Me you may have peace...."*

Your peace is not in this world. It has nothing to do with the amount of money or life insurance you possess. Your security is in the assurance of God's holy Word. God's peace *"...surpasses all understanding..."* (Phil. 4:7).

If Jesus has overcome the world, then you are a world overcomer because He lives in you. If Jesus said you would have peace, then peace is yours. If Jesus said to be of good cheer, then be of good cheer.

Be joyful, and do not allow circumstances to rob your happiness and joy. Be at peace and full of joy because you are an overcomer. In the midst of the worst tribulation or difficulty, you *can* stand immovable as you trust in God's Word.

DECLARATION OF FAITH

I am in Jesus, and Jesus is in me.
I have overcome since Jesus has overcome.
The peace of God rules my life.
Joy dominates my life. I am an overcomer.
I always triumph in Jesus.

— 81 —

You Know All Things

But you have an anointing from the
Holy One, and you know all things.

1 JOHN 2:20

You have been anointed by the Spirit of God to know the truth. The unction or anointing of the Holy Spirit gives revelation knowledge of the things of God.

God has given you His Holy Spirit so you might know everything there is to know about Him. You can know God personally.

As Jesus walked on the road to Emmaus with two of the disciples, He talked to them about the Scriptures concerning Himself. Later, Jesus appeared to them in a home where all of the disciples had met. He *"...opened their understanding, that they might comprehend the Scriptures"* (Luke 24:45). When He did this, the light of revelation knowledge flooded their understanding.

The anointing of the Holy Spirit opens your understanding so you can comprehend the deep mysteries of the kingdom of God. Jesus said, *"And you shall know the truth, and the truth shall make you free"* (John 8:32). The anointing of the Spirit of God is upon you to give you the full knowledge of the truth. You hold the keys to your freedom.

"But the Helper, the Holy Spirit, whom the Father will send in My name, He will teach you all things, and bring to your remembrance all things that I said to you" (John 14:26).

The Holy Spirit resides in you to teach you all things concerning the kingdom of God. You have all the advantages, for the best teacher there is dwells in you. *Whatever you need to know, He will teach you.*

DECLARATION OF FAITH

I am anointed by the Spirit of God. He teaches me everything I need to know. I see and understand the truth, for the Holy Spirit leads me into all truth.

— 82 —

The Love Walk

He who loves his brother abides in the light,
and there is no cause for stumbling in him.

1 JOHN 2:10

There is divine protection for you when you walk in love with others. To walk in love is to walk in the light. When you get nasty and ugly with people, the light goes out.

Years ago, a couple started coming to our church. The wife was going after God wholeheartedly. She was seeking Him, and believing and confessing God's Word. Her husband, on the other hand, was dragging his feet. He was a businessman. He read his Bible, prayed, and came to church when he could. But he was not on the same spiritual level as his wife. Since he worked late on Saturday nights, many times he would sleep in on Sunday mornings and miss the 11:00 service, which his wife and children attended.

One Saturday, the wife told her husband she would save him a seat at the 11:00 service, then they would go out to eat afterwards. He didn't show up for the 11:00 service, and the wife became angry on the inside. She was upset and in strife with him. After the service, she saw her husband in the parking lot, smiling, happy, and ready to go to lunch. She responded with anger towards him. As she was driving to the restaurant, she was involved in a car accident.

She later prayed, "Lord, I do not understand. I'm tithing, and You said You would rebuke the devourer for my sake. I am praising You, and You said You would stop the enemy if I praised You. I am confessing the Word...."

The Lord interrupted her and said, "Your strife opened the door to the enemy." (James 3:14-16.)

Faith works by love; and when you get out of love, your faith ceases to work.

This woman asked God, "What do I do?"

He said, "Love your husband, pray for him, minister to him, and bless him."

She followed the Lord's instruction; and today, Janet and Bill Lay pastor Cornerstone Church in Grove, Oklahoma. Bill answered the call to ministry because his wife loved him into the place where God had destined him to be.

Love is the best way. It will work for you in any situation.

DECLARATION OF FAITH

Because I choose to walk in the God-kind of love,
or agape love, my faith works. As a result,
I walk in victory in every area of life.

— 83 —

Jesus Christ—
Always the Same

Jesus Christ is the same yesterday, today, and forever.

HEBREWS 13:8

Jesus never changes. He is eternally constant. You can know with complete assurance that He will enforce the Word of God, for He never veers from it. Since Jesus victoriously triumphed over Satan at the Cross, you can always count on Him to be victorious.

"For I am the Lord, I do not change..." (Mal. 3:6). Defeat is not a part of God's nature. He is successful in everything that He wants accomplished on the earth. Through the blood of Jesus, you are united with the life of God. You, therefore, can live in the same victory that is part of God's nature.

Most Christians who do not have a firm foundation of the Word of God in their hearts live "roller coaster lives." They go up and down moment by moment with each obstacle and trial that faces them. Without knowing the character of God or what His Word says, many think this "roller coaster experience" is normal. This type of thinking couldn't be further from the truth.

God wants you to live a constant life of victory. Your constancy is based on His record. If you always stand on His Word and never veer from what it says, you won't change either. Like God, you will live in a position of constant triumph and victory.

Your steadfast confession is what will put you over. When you use the authority that Jesus gave you, you can speak to any mountain of adversity and watch it crumble before you. Bad circumstances don't have to disturb you when your trust is in the Word.

Jesus Christ is still the same. The victory He obtained over the devil is still in effect. Satan has not won back any territory since his defeat. Stand firm in the victory Christ has obtained for you.

DECLARATION OF FAITH

Since God and Jesus never change, I won't change my position of victory. I will always stand on the Word, which guarantees my victory. Through the Word, I am consistent, constant, and steadfast. I always triumph in Christ.

— 84 —

Far From Oppression

In righteousness you shall be established;
you shall be far from oppression, for you shall not fear;
and from terror, for it shall not come near you.

ISAIAH 54:14

I n the above verse, God says, *"...you shall be...."* He
believes in you and His power to work through you.
You can believe in yourself because God believes in
you. Since He said you are established in righteousness,
you should believe His Word.

Righteousness is right standing with God. When you
are in right standing with God, you should not experience
any sense of guilt, condemnation, or inferiority when you
approach His throne.

Righteousness is not something you earn. You can
only receive it by faith. *"For He made Him who knew no sin to
be sin for us, that we might become the righteousness of God in
Him"* (2 Cor. 5:21).

You are righteous by faith in Jesus Christ. God no longer condemns you. You are forgiven. Though your sins were as scarlet, they are now as white as snow through the blood of Jesus. (Isa. 1:18.) As far as the east is from the west, God has removed your sin. (Ps. 103:12.) God sees you as the righteousness of Him in Christ. (2 Cor. 5:21.)

Since God no longer looks at your sin, the accuser of the brethren has no place to condemn you because God has declared you righteous. *"Who shall bring a charge against God's elect? It is God who justifies"* (Rom. 8:33).

No wonder you are far from oppression. Satan wouldn't dare get close to God's righteousness. You don't have to have any fear because *"If God is for [you], who can be against [you]?"* (Rom. 8:31).

Nothing can overcome God, and you have God on your side. He is with you every day, guarding and protecting you.

When you are established and fully settled in God's righteousness, fear no longer has a place in you. In essence, righteousness is like a fortress that surrounds you and keeps torment and oppression far from you.

DECLARATION OF FAITH

I am the righteousness of God.
The Word has set me free from fear and oppression.
They have no place in my life because God is for me.
I live without worry, anxiety, and heaviness because
I am established in righteousness.

— 85 —

Victory Over Depression, Grief, and Sorrow

Surely [Jesus] has borne our griefs and carried
our sorrows; yet we esteemed Him stricken,
smitten by God, and afflicted.
But He was wounded for our transgressions, He was
bruised for our iniquities; the chastisement for our
peace was upon Him, and by His stripes we are healed.

ISAIAH 53:4,5

The wounds that Jesus bore on His back had a two-fold purpose. His blood was shed not only for our sins but for our sicknesses as well. Many times when people pray for healing, they don't have a basis for their faith. They are *hoping* God will hear their prayer and do something. They don't have any confidence that He hears them and answers their prayers.

Jesus' blood heals all diseases, and that includes mental illnesses as well. I read the story of a man in a mental institution who had lost all hope. His mind was completely gone, and his life devastated. In addition, many people in mental institutions are so heavily medicated that their problems are compounded.

This man was so mentally depressed that he felt like he was sinking into hell. One of the doctor's names in his ward was "Heven" [pronounced heaven]. However, when he heard Dr. Heven's name being called, all he heard was "heaven."

A thought went through his mind: *If I am in heaven, I am not in hell.* He finally had a ray of hope. He reasoned that if he wasn't in hell, then he wasn't lost. He eventually left the institution and committed his life to Christ. Years later, he shared his testimony of deliverance. One little spark of hope turned his life around.

Jesus is still in the healing business today and wants to set you free. Receive His healing oil of joy for mourning and heaviness. The garment of praise is available to you to conquer depression. (Isa. 61:1-3.)

Today is a new day for you as you receive your inheritance of healing and wholeness that Jesus provided for you in His death, burial, and resurrection.

DECLARATION OF FAITH

I can walk in victory because God has given me power, love, and a sound mind. (2 Tim. 1:7.) I, therefore, refuse to entertain thoughts of depression, grief, and sorrow.

— 86 —

Blessed

"Now it shall come to pass, if you diligently obey the voice of the Lord your God, to observe carefully all His commandments which I command you today, that the Lord your God will set you high above all nations of the earth. "And all these blessings shall come upon you and overtake you, because you obey the voice of the Lord your God."

DEUTERONOMY 28:1,2

A s you follow after the commandments of God, you can expect the blessings listed in Deuteronomy 28 to follow after you. When you do your part, God will do His part.

"If you are willing and obedient, you shall eat the good of the land" (Isa. 1:19). We can see in the history of the Israelites, which is outlined in the books of Kings, Chronicles, and Samuel, that when Israelites followed after God, His blessings were upon them and they lived in peace. When they forsook His ways and worshipped idols, His blessings were removed from their lives.

Living under the blessings of God is as simple as making a decision to follow Him fully. When you do, the course of your life is set. The blessings are yours now. God said that *if* you have met the condition, you can expect His goodness and mercy to follow you. As a result:

You have been set above all the nations of the earth.

You are blessed above all people.

The blessings of God overtake you.

You are blessed in the city and in the field. (Deut. 28:3.)

You are blessed coming and going. (v. 6.)

Your enemies flee before you. (v. 7.)

Your storehouses and everything you undertake are blessed. (v. 8.)

You have a *"...surplus of prosperity...."* (v. 11 AMP.)

You are the head and not the tail, above only and not beneath. (v. 13.)

DECLARATION OF FAITH

Since I follow after God, I am blessed in every way.
God's blessings are upon me in abundance.
Everything I do prospers.
I am willing and obedient, and I eat the good of the land.

— 87 —

Satisfied With Good Things

Bless the Lord, O my soul; and all that is
within me, bless His holy name!
Bless the Lord, O my soul, and forget not all His benefits:
Who forgives all your iniquities,
who heals all your diseases,
Who redeems your life from destruction, who crowns
you with lovingkindness and tender mercies,
Who satisfies your mouth with good things,
so that your youth is renewed like the eagle's.

PSALM 103:1-5

You are blessed. God has loaded you with benefits that are not available to this world. They are pleasures that only come to the children of God.

Through Jesus, your sins are forgiven. You no longer experience condemnation, guilt, shame, or punishment. Your past is forgotten; your sins are covered by the blood of Jesus.

Jesus, the Great Physician, has healed all your diseases. No more cancer, ulcers, or heart failure. Divine life and health pulsate through your body.

Abundant life is your daily portion. You have been redeemed from destruction. Calamity is a thing of the past. It may happen to those around you, but it will not come "nigh you." Disaster is off limits to your household. You have a supernatural 24-hour security service, provided by the Trinity.

Lovingkindness and mercy crown your life. Anger, strife, animosity, torment, and worry are gone. God has filled you with Himself.

Thank God for the good things that He has provided for you. You have a good heavenly Father who has already blessed you with many spiritual as well as natural blessings.

DECLARATION OF FAITH

I am blessed with many good things.
Through the blood of Jesus, my sins are forgiven.
Jesus has healed me of all diseases. I am filled and
surrounded with the kind mercies of God.
My life is redeemed from destruction.
I rejoice in the many benefits of the Lord.

— 88 —

Prosperous and Successful

"This Book of the Law shall not depart from your mouth,
but you shall meditate in it day and night, that you may
observe to do according to all that is written in it.
For then you will make your way prosperous,
and then you will have good success."

JOSHUA 1:8

The Father wants you to be prosperous and success-ful. While the world has its ideas about prosperity and success, they are only counterfeits. God's pros-perity and success cover your spirit, soul, body, family, work, and finances; in other words, every part of your being and every part of your life.

God has given you His Word so you are strong spiri-tually. There are promises in the Word that cover every-thing that you will ever experience. The Word fills any feelings of emptiness and removes all fear. He has also

183

given you the Holy Spirit from which the forces of life flow from your heart.

As you renew your mind to the Word, vile imaginations and agitating illusions can no longer torment you. You have direct access to the source of *all* knowledge. You have the mind of Christ and know all things. (1 Cor. 2:16; 1 John 2:20.)

The Word also provides healing and strength for your body. (1 Peter 2:24; Isa. 40:31.) All of your needs are met in the Word. (Phil. 4:19.)

As you make the Word your daily bread by meditating on it, talking about it, and acting on it, you will experience the same success and abundance that was promised to Joshua.

Prosperity and success are the by-products of living in God. They are the result of the Word being first place in your life. They are the rewards for seeking after God. When Jesus is the object of your love and obedience, prosperity and success are natural by-products.

DECLARATION OF FAITH

*Meditating on God's Word is a priority in my life.
I meditate on the truth constantly and do not allow
anything to distract me from my time with the Lord.
I am willing and obedient; and as a result, I eat the good
of the land. I am prosperous and successful
because God's kingdom is first in my life.*

— 89 —

Jesus Has All Power

*And Jesus came and spoke to them, saying, "All
authority has been given to Me in heaven and on earth."*

MATTHEW 28:18

S ince Jesus has *all* power in heaven and earth, you can
be fearless because He lives in you. He has all power,
all authority—in heaven and earth. The devil has
been stripped of the power or authority he gained in the fall
of Adam. Ignorance of Jesus' triumph at the resurrection
has held millions in slavery. You, however, have the truth—
so tell the world!

Through His death, Jesus destroyed the one *"...who
had the power of death, that is, the devil"* (Heb. 2:14). The word
destroyed is translated *"paralyzed, brought to nought, and
defeated."* In addition, Jesus *"...disarmed principalities and powers,
He made a public spectacle of them, triumphing over them in it"*
(Col. 2:15).

Jesus disarmed Satan and his demon forces. He
stripped them of their authority, power, and dominion. He

made an open, public display of their defeat. Since you are a follower of Christ, you have every reason to walk in *victory* here and now in this life.

Jesus said, *"I am he that liveth, and was dead; and, behold, I am alive for evermore, Amen; and have the keys of hell and of death"* (Rev. 1:18 KJV).

Jesus has the keys of hell and of death. Satan can no longer hold you in bondage. Fear and death cannot dominate you.

Instead, *you* dominate the devil! *You* command unclean spirits to leave. *You* set the captives free. *You* lay hands on the sick and see them recover and be delivered. Nothing can stop *you*. You walk in the authority and power of Jesus Christ—the King of kings and the Lord of lords.

DECLARATION OF FAITH

Jesus lives in me. He has all authority.
When I exercise His authority, men are set free.
Through the blood of Jesus, the sick are healed,
devils are cast out, and the oppressed are set free.
I proclaim liberty to the captives, and they are set free.

— 90 —

Take the Lid Off!

Jesus said, "If you can believe,
all things are possible to him who believes."

Faith is how we receive all of the promises of God.
It is also how we fulfill His plan for our lives.
Any inkling of doubt and fear will hinder our
faith and keep us from receiving.

In Mark 9, a father brought his mute son to the
disciples so he might be delivered. However, they could
not help him. The man said to Jesus, *"...I spoke to Your disci-*
ples, that they should cast [the mute spirit] out, but they could not"
(Mark 9:18).

Imagine the father's discouragement. When he got to
Jesus he said, *"...If You can do anything, have compassion on us*
and help us" (Mark 9:22). God not only has the power to
heal, He also has the willingness and the compassion to
deliver you. The gospels are filled with instances where

Jesus was moved with compassion. Mercy, compassion, and love are expressions of the very essence and nature of God.

However, faith is how you bring healing from the spiritual realm into the natural realm. Jesus put the responsibility on the father when He said, *"If you can believe, all things are possible to him who believes"* (v. 23). Jesus wasn't judging the father; instead, He was spurring the father to act in faith, so his son could be healed.

Think of it this way. You can have a huge water tower and plenty of water pressure at your house, but unless you turn on the water faucet, no water is going to come out. That is the way it is with faith. Your faith must be switched on. Turn on your faith faucet so it is wide open. When you do, you will be able to receive by faith the promises of God.

The father of the mute child said, *"...Lord, I believe; help my unbelief!"* (v. 24). This is an example of how you can have faith in your heart but doubt in your head. What is important, however, is what is in your heart. Because the father had faith in his heart, Jesus rebuked the spirit and the boy was delivered. (vv. 25-27.)

Keep your faith faucet wide open, and watch what God will do for you.

DECLARATION OF FAITH

I remove limitation from my thinking and my faith.
I keep my faith faucet turned wide open.
As a result, I receive the end of my faith.

— 91 —

Perfect Love

There is no fear in love; but perfect love
casts out fear, because fear involves torment.
But he who fears has not been made perfect in love.

1 JOHN 4:18

The moment you were born again, you were filled with the love of God. (Rom. 5:5.) We know that *"...love is of God; and everyone who loves is born of God and knows God"* (1 John 4:7).

God is love, and He dwells in you. As a new creation in Christ, you have been made in the likeness and image of love. You have love in you; it is now your nature.

Obedience to God through keeping His Word causes the love inside of you to mature and develop. *"But whoever keeps His word, truly the love of God is perfected in him. By this we know that we are in Him"* (1 John 2:5).

As a doer of the Word, you have made the decision to obey God. Whatever He desires becomes your delight; you are willing and obedient to obey His commands.

Since love is your new nature, hate and anger cannot be a part of you. If anybody slanders your name or twists your words, the love in your heart forgives that person. Love returns kindness to those who strike at you to destroy your happiness.

The love in your heart drives out fear. Fear of sickness, poverty, or sin can no longer hold you in bondage, for you know what Jesus has provided for you in the plan of redemption.

The love of God also drives out any fear of people because you are no longer concerned about what others think. You love them just the same whether they like you or not.

DECLARATION OF FAITH

I am born of love. Love fills my very being.
The fruit of the Spirit in me is love. Perfect love
has cast out all fear. No worry or anxiety can come
into my life because God's love reigns supreme.
I am fearless and loving in every circumstance.

— 92 —

Every Good Thing

*For the Lord God is a sun and shield; the Lord
will give grace and glory; no good thing will He
withhold from those who walk uprightly.*

PSALM 84:11

You are the righteousness of God and walk uprightly. For you, there is no other way to live. Since you are sold out and totally committed to Jesus, God promises to withhold no good thing from you.

Your Father is so loving. He has given you everything that pertains to life and godliness, through the knowledge of Jesus Christ. (2 Peter 1:3.)

Jesus came to give you abundant life. (John 10:10.) He is the Good Shepherd who leads you into green pastures and causes your cup to run over. (Ps. 23.) You have more than enough of everything you need.

"Every good gift and every perfect gift is from above, and comes down from the Father of lights, with whom there is no variation or shadow of turning" (James 1:17).

You are blessed with every spiritual blessing. (Eph. 1:3.) God supplies everything you need according to His riches in glory by Christ Jesus. (Phil. 4:19.)

You do not even need to think about yourself. The kingdom of God is first in your life, and *"...all these things..."* are added to you (Matt. 6:33). You are, therefore, free to be a blessing to others.

There is no concern about what life may bring. You have everything you need to overcome any attack of the devil: the name of Jesus, the blood of Jesus, the Word of God, and the word of your testimony. You know without a shadow of a doubt that God will never withhold any good thing from you, and you rest in His love.

DECLARATION OF FAITH

The Lord is my Shepherd, and I do not lack.
No good thing is withheld from me because I walk uprightly.
I want for nothing. I have everything in Christ Jesus.
The blessings of God have overtaken me, and
my cup runs over. All of my needs are supplied.

— 93 —

Shall Not Want

The Lord is my shepherd; I shall not want.

PSALM 23:1

This is your confession: *The Lord Jesus Christ is my Shepherd*. He said, *"I am the good shepherd..."* (John 10:14). The Good Shepherd came to give you abundant life. *Abundance* means "more than adequate."

The first miracle Jesus performed was when He turned water into wine. He changed 150 gallons of water into premium wine for a wedding party. Think of it. Jesus provided 150 gallons of wine for a group of less than 100 people—in all probability—at the end of a wedding feast.

One day Jesus borrowed Peter's boat so He could teach a crowd of people. Afterward He told Peter to launch out into the deep and let his nets down for a catch of fish. They caught so many fish that the boat almost sank! Whenever Jesus did something, it was *always* more than enough.

Remember the loaves and fish? In Matthew 14, Jesus fed 5,000 people and had 12 basketfuls left over. Later, in Matthew 15, He fed 4,000 and had 7 baskets of leftovers. Jesus is the Good Shepherd. He takes care of His flock and abundantly supplies. You are being supplied according to His riches in glory. (Phil. 4:19.) There is more than enough in heaven. You will never break heaven's bank account with any of your needs or requests.

God satisfies your mouth with good things. (Ps. 103:5.) In fact, He will withhold no good thing from you. (Ps. 84:11.)

DECLARATION OF FAITH

The Lord is my Shepherd; I shall not want.
God supplies all of my needs according to
His riches in glory by Christ Jesus. I lack for nothing.
I have more than enough of everything I need for
my spirit, soul, and body. Jesus is my everything.
In Him I have life more abundantly.

— 94 —

Angels at Work for You

For He shall give His angels charge over you,
to keep you in all your ways.

PSALM 91:11

The word *keep* means "to guard, protect, and deliver."

Psalm 103:20 says, *"Bless the Lord, you His angels, who excel in strength, who do His word, heeding the voice of His word."* When you speak aloud the promises of God's Word, the angels hearken to the voice of the Word of God that is coming from your lips.

When you say, *"The Lord is my refuge and my fortress"* (Ps. 91:2), the angels move on your behalf. They act on the Word you declare. If you don't speak the Word (or words that align with God's Word), even though you are a believer, their wings remain folded. Angels are not released to do your bidding until you speak the Word.

Years ago, I was driving down Highway 169, headed toward I-244 in Tulsa. Around Mingo and Admiral, the highway takes a giant loop and goes over the interstate. There is a big grassy area where it curves and turns toward the airport.

As I was going around that curve, a car passed me. Now I was going the speed limit when he passed me, so he must have been going 90 to 100 miles an hour. As he sped by, I felt compassion for him. I cried out, "God, save him," because I could tell that something was wrong. In a flash in my mind, I saw my angels on the front of my car. I said, "Angels, go get him!"

He missed the curve and went over the embankment. When he hit the grass, his car rolled several times. I pulled to the side of the road, jumped out, and ran toward his car which landed in an upright position. The guy was sitting in the backseat, looking out the window at me. I said, "Man, God just saved your life." He said, "I know it." I prayed for him to receive the Lord right there.

Angels will work for you when you speak God's Word.

DECLARATION OF FAITH

Angels are watching over me. As I believe and speak the promises of God's Word, they go forth to perform the Word. The Lord is my refuge and my fortress. He delivers me from tragedy, calamity, disaster, and disease, in Jesus' name.

— 95 —

Planted in a Local Church

Those who are planted in the house of the Lord
shall flourish in the courts of our God.

PSALM 92:13

A re you planted in a local church where you are receiving input, ministry, training, and discipleship to mature you spiritually? God didn't save you for you to sit back and do nothing for the kingdom of God. He saved you for a specific purpose, a special assignment.

If you have been delivered out of a swamp, do you walk away from the screams of others who are still drowning in that same swamp? One of the worst things about the sinking of the Titanic was that hundreds of people in life jackets died in the water because the people who were in lifeboats refused to help them. In the same way, many people who have been saved from the flames of hell aren't doing anything to rescue anyone else. They are only thinking of themselves.

When God saved you, He didn't want you to shut your ears to the cries of the drowning. He saved you so you would lift someone else out of the murky waters. Being involved in a local church and its evangelism outreaches is a great way to help others.

Here are ways you can be planted in a local church:

Attending. (Heb. 10:24,25.)

Praying for one another. (Eph. 6:18.)

Giving of your finances. (Mal. 3:8-11.)

Serving. (1 Cor. 12:14-26.)

God needs your commitment, and the body of Christ needs you. When you realize that God has placed you in a particular church and He has a work for you to do, you won't become a holy "roamer" if you become disgruntled. You will stay put and flourish in that house of God.

DECLARATION OF FAITH

I am planted in a local church where I attend regularly,
I pray for others, I give of my finances, and I serve with the
love of God. I am flourishing in the blessing of the Lord.

— 96 —

Why Pray in Tongues?

*"Go into all the world and preach
the gospel to every creature.*
*"He who believes and is baptized will be saved;
but he who does not believe will be condemned.*
*"And these signs will follow those who believe:
In my name...they will speak with new tongues."*

MARK 16:15-17

The gift of the Holy Spirit with the evidence of speaking in other tongues follows the salvation experience. First Corinthians 14:4 says, *"He who speaks in a tongue edifies himself...."* To *edify* means "to strengthen or to build up your inner man."

When I transferred to Oral Roberts University during the second semester of my sophomore year, the baptism with the Holy Spirit with the evidence of praying in other tongues was not a part of my life. I read the book *They Speak with Other Tongues* by John Sherrill, and it answered my questions about tongues.

Later, I attended a church that taught on the baptism of the Holy Spirit. When the pastor asked, "How many want to receive the baptism of the Holy Spirit?" I raised my hand because now I understood why I needed to pray in tongues. Before anyone could lay hands on me, I began speaking in tongues.

When Jesus said, *"He that believeth on me, as the scripture hath said, out of his belly shall flow rivers of living water"* (John 7:38 KJV), He was speaking about the Holy Spirit.

The baptism of the Holy Spirit, with the evidence of speaking in other tongues and interpreting your tongues, will quicken your mind. As the Spirit of God flows through you, He generates power in your life, helping you to live in victory. *You need God's power flowing through you.*

DECLARATION OF FAITH

I will build myself up on my most holy faith every day
by praying in the Holy Spirit and interpreting what
I speak in other tongues. (Jude 20; 1 Cor. 14:13.)

Whatever You Do Shall Prosper

Blessed is the man who walks not in the counsel of
the ungodly, nor stands in the path of sinners,
nor sits in the seat of the scornful;
But his delight is in the law of the Lord,
and in His law he meditates day and night.
He shall be like a tree planted by the rivers of water, that
brings forth its fruit in its season, whose leaf also shall
not wither; and whatever he does shall prosper.

PSALM 1:1-3

These verses praise the person who walks in the counsel of God instead of seeking advice from those who don't know the Lord. This individual makes his delight in the things of the Lord instead of what the world seeks after. Because of the person's decision to go after God, the blessings of God rest on him and everything he does prospers.

It doesn't matter what is happening in the world. When you seek after God, you become like a tree that is planted by rivers of living water. The entire world may be in a drought, but your roots go down deep into the rivers of living water. You are not affected by any world crises, just as a tree planted by the river is not affected by a long, hot summer.

These verses paint a picture of someone who is abiding in Christ. As a result, the individual bears much fruit and receives answers to prayer. (John 15:7,8.)

Whatever you do prospers, and everything you touch is blessed when you have made God your priority. He guides your steps and shows you which pathway to take. Because you have made Him the central focus of your life, He gives you the desires of your heart.

You then become an obvious testimony of God's goodness and faithfulness. While others fail and faint under the trials, tribulations, and persecution, you continue to be blessed and to be a blessing.

God's Word works. You have discovered the key to be an overcomer—*God's Word.*

DECLARATION OF FAITH

I am a doer of the Word. I am blessed in my deeds. I meditate in the Word day and night, and I am like a tree planted by rivers of living water. Whatever I do prospers because God is involved in my life. My life continually bears good fruit.

— 98 —

Winning People
to the Lord

The fruit of the righteous is a tree of life,
and he who wins souls is wise.

PROVERBS 11:30

Y ou have been saved to help other people get saved. You have been delivered to help others get delivered. You have been rescued from hell to become a rescuer of others and set them on a pathway that leads to heaven. Soul-winning is not the responsibility of a designated few—the minister, the missionary, or the evangelist. Everyone is called to win the lost.

Soul-winning is a huge issue to Jesus because He gave His blood so people could be won into the kingdom of God. It is a big issue with God, because He gave His Son to die on the Cross. Jesus came to the earth as a soul-winner because He saw the value of human beings.

We have an Iranian church within our congregation that meets every Sunday morning. The entire service is in Farsi, the primary language of the Iranian people. This group is pastored by a man who, at one time, was a staunch Moslem.

The Iranian minister also started a church in Oklahoma City and one in Phoenix, Arizona. Before he was saved, he persecuted Christians. One day a friend told him about Jesus. He found out the name of the person who witnessed to his friend and wrote him: "If you ever try to witness to any of our people again, I will strap a bomb on my body and blow you up!" The American who had witnessed to his friend wrote him back and shared the love of God with him. A few weeks later, this Moslem had a dream where Jesus appeared to him with outstretched arms. Our Iranian minister gave his life to Christ.

How did this happen? Someone dared to step out of their comfort zone and share the truth of the gospel of Jesus Christ with him. It's time for you and me to do the same. Let's get out of our comfort zones and go after the lost!

DECLARATION OF FAITH

*As a part of my daily lifestyle, I am pursuing
souls for God's kingdom. I have the call to go.
The love of God is in my heart to rescue as
many people as possible from the depths of hell.
The message of the Cross will set them free.
I will share the good news of Jesus everywhere I go.*

— 99 —

Jesus Has Opened Heaven to You!

"...Did I not say to you that if you would believe you would see the glory of God?"

JOHN 11:40

J esus came that you might have life in all of its fullness. He came to bring light into the dark places of your life. He came to remove every barrier of sin and to pay the penalty for your iniquities. He suffered in your place so you could have eternal life. The curse has been lifted and heaven has been opened to you because of Jesus' death, burial, and resurrection. In other words, heaven's blessings have been released to you. Jesus has opened heaven to you.

So what is the blessing? It is God Himself. Jesus said, *"...He who has seen Me has seen the Father..."* (John 14:9). When you receive Jesus as Lord and Savior, you receive the blessing because Jesus is the Blessed One. In Him is life. Christianity is about a *relationship* with Jesus Christ—it's not about a code, a dogma, a set of rules, or rituals. You have God in you through the indwelling presence of His Spirit.

When you mix faith with God's Word, the miracle from heaven you need will be manifested to you.

A few years ago, a young lady came to our church. Melissa not only was bound with drugs and alcohol, she also was anorexic. She was skin and bones—a mere 94 pounds. She didn't have a car, a job, or a place to live. She was headed on a pathway of destruction. When she was introduced to Jesus Christ, she accepted Him as her Lord, Savior, and Deliverer. Her captivity was turned.

Jesus opened heaven to her. The glory of God manifested in her life. Today, she is healed, she has a job, a car, and a place to live. Now her life is fruitful for the kingdom of God.

Jesus will open heaven to you as you surrender to His lordship and seek Him daily with all of your heart.

DECLARATION OF FAITH

I receive Jesus, the Blessed One, into my life.
By my acceptance of Him and total surrender to Him,
the curse is stopped from affecting me, and God's glory
manifests in my life. I am living under His open heaven.

— 100 —

Greater Is He

You are of God, little children, and
have overcome them, because He who is
in you is greater than he who is in the world.

1 JOHN 4:4

When you made Jesus the Lord of your life, you became filled with the very life of God and became a partaker of His divine nature. As a child of God, you are an heir of God and have a right to everything that is His. You have already overcome because the Overcomer dwells in you.

Jesus is greater than the devil. He defeated him at the Cross of Calvary. He is greater than sin, sickness, or poverty. Jesus is greater than any weapon formed against you.

For Joshua, God was greater than the walls of Jericho. (Josh. 6:20.)

For David, God was greater than Goliath. (1 Sam. 17:49.)

For the three Hebrew boys, God was greater than the fiery furnace. (Dan. 3:26.)

For Moses, God was greater than the Egyptian army and the Red Sea. (Ex. 14:21-27.)

For Noah, God was greater than the flood. (Gen. 6:17,18.)

For Daniel, God was greater than lions. (Dan. 6:22.)

For Paul and Silas, God was greater than chains and prison doors. (Acts 16:26.)

For Bartimaeus, Jesus was greater than blindness. (Mark 10:52.)

For the woman caught in adultery, Jesus was greater than her sin. (John 8:11.)

For the demoniac, Jesus was greater than the demons. (Mark 5:8-13.)

For the leper, Jesus was greater than leprosy. (Matt. 8:3.)

For the disciples, Jesus was greater than the storm. (Matt. 8:26.)

For Lazarus, Jesus was greater than death. (John 11:43,44.)

For you—Jesus is greater than the devil and everything he has!

DECLARATION OF FAITH

Greater is Jesus in me than the devil in the world.
I am filled with the spirit of power.
Divine life flows through me.
No weapon formed against me prospers.
I have overcome. I am victorious.
Jesus is greater than all the works of the devil.
I am fearless in Jesus.

— 101 —

Spiritual Terrorist Status: HIGH ALERT!

But concerning the times and the seasons, brethren,

you have no need that I should write to you.

For you yourselves know perfectly that the day

of the Lord so comes as a thief in the night....

But you, brethren, are not in darkness, so that

this Day should overtake you as a thief....

But let us who are of the day be sober,

putting on the breastplate of faith and love,

and as a helmet the hope of salvation.

1 THESSALONIANS 5:1,2,4,8

The coming of the Lord should not catch you unaware. You are not D.U.I. (driving under the influence) of the spirit of the world, the lust of the flesh, or demonic desires. There are people who are not intoxicated with alcohol but with their own desires. They are under the influence of selfishness and are pursuing something that is totally opposite of what God has planned for their lives.

To be alert and watchful in this hour means we must be faith people: faith believing, faith talking, faith thinking, and faith acting.

It is not "business as usual" today, either naturally or spiritually. Satan, the original terrorist, knows that his time is short. The Bible tells us that in the last days he will come with great fury (or anger) against the people of God. Revelation 12:12 confirms this: *"...For the devil has come down to you, having great wrath, because he knows that he has a short time."* We are in this season right now.

When Paul speaks of the "last days," he is talking about the appearing of the Lord Jesus Christ for His Church—the Rapture and all the events leading to it and following that event. We are in this time period right now. You can still live in victory every day of your life by being watchful and sober.

DECLARATION OF FAITH

I am on high alert spiritually and naturally through daily prayer and input of God's Word. I choose to walk in absolute victory through my faith in Jesus.

Prayer of Salvation

God loves you—no matter who you are, no matter what your past. God loves you so much that He gave His one and only begotten Son for you. The Bible tells us that "...whoever believes in him shall not perish but have eternal life" (John 3:16 NIV). Jesus laid down His life and rose again so that we could spend eternity with Him in heaven and experience His absolute best on earth. If you would like to receive Jesus into your life, pray the following prayer out loud and mean it from your heart.

> *Heavenly Father, I come to You admitting that I am a sinner. Right now, I choose to turn away from sin, and I ask You to cleanse me of all unrighteousness. I believe that Your Son, Jesus, died on the Cross to take away my sins. I also believe that He rose again from the dead so that I might be forgiven of my sins and made righteous through faith in Him. I call upon the name of Jesus Christ to be the Savior and Lord of my life. Jesus, I choose to follow You and ask that You fill me with the power of the Holy Spirit. I declare that right now I am a child of God. I am free from sin and full of the righteousness of God. I am saved in Jesus' name. Amen.*

If you prayed this prayer to receive Jesus Christ as your Savior for the first time, please contact us on the Web at **www.harrisonhouse.com** or **www.victory.com** to receive a free book.

Or you may write to us at

Harrison House
P.O. Box 35035
Tulsa, Oklahoma 74153

or

Victory Christian Center
7700 S. Lewis
Tulsa, Oklahoma 74136

About the Author

Billy Joe Daugherty, along with his wife, Sharon, founded and pastor Victory Christian Center, a church of more than 14,000 members in Tulsa, Oklahoma. Ministries of the church include Victory Christian School, a K3-12 program with more than 1,300 students; a daycare program with over 300 infants and preschoolers; Victory Bible Institute, which provides ministerial training both in the classroom and online, as well as 273 International Victory Bible Institutes in 65 countries with more than 9,000 students; *Word Explosion,* a major inspirational and training event that draws close to 20,000 participants each year; and *Victory in Jesus,* a daily television broadcast hosted by Billy Joe and Sharon.

To contact Billy Joe Daugherty
please write to:

Victory Christian Center
7700 S. Lewis
Tulsa, Oklahoma 74136
Phone: 918-491-7700

Or visit him on the Web at:
www.victory.com

What Happens When
Life on Earth Is Over?

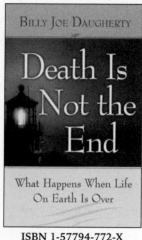

ISBN 1-57794-772-X

What hope is there for a loved one who has died? And what hope is there for those who mourn their passing away? In this book of peace and comfort, Pastor Billy Joe Daugherty reminds believers—and provides a powerful resource to put into the hands of one who is experiencing deep loss—of Jesus' profound words of a future home to His disciples.

Daugherty weaves together simple insights, Bible verses, and prayers to assure readers that death is not the final word for those who love God. Jesus has prepared a place for them in heaven.

Available at bookstores everywhere
or visit **www.harrisonhouse.com**.

www.harrisonhouse.com

Fast. Easy. Convenient!

- ◆ New Book Information
- ◆ Look Inside the Book
- ◆ Press Releases
- ◆ Bestsellers
- ◆ Free E-News
- ◆ Author Biographies

- ◆ Upcoming Books
- ◆ Share Your Testimony
- ◆ Online Product Availability
- ◆ Product Specials
- ◆ Order Online

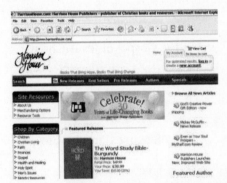

For the latest in book news and author information, please visit us on the Web at www.harrisonhouse.com. Get up-to-date pictures and details on all our powerful and life-changing products. Sign up for our e-mail newsletter, *Friends of the House,* and receive free monthly information on our authors and products including testimonials, author announcements, and more!

Harrison House—
Books That Bring Hope, Books That Bring Change

Harrison House Vision

Proclaiming the truth and the power

Of the Gospel of Jesus Christ

With excellence;

Challenging Christians to

Live victoriously,

Grow spiritually,

Know God intimately.